MUSIC

IDEAS IN PROFILE
SMALL INTRODUCTIONS TO BIG TOPICS

ALSO BY ANDREW GANT

Christmas Carols: From Village Green to Church Choir

O Sing unto the Lord: A History of English Church Music

MUSIC

ANDREW GANT

P

PROFILE BOOKS

First published in Great Britain in 2017 by
PROFILE BOOKS LTD
3 Holford Yard
Bevin Way
London WC1X 9HD
www.profilebooks.com

10 9 8 7 6 5 4 3 2 1

A CIP catalogue record for this book is available from the British Library.

ISBN 978 1 78125 642 8

eISBN 978 1 78283 251 5

Designed by Jade Design *www.jadedesign.co.uk*

Printed and bound in Italy by L.E.G.O. S.p.A.

CONTENTS

INTRODUCTION   1

PART I: WHAT IS MUSIC?
   1. What is music?   9
   2. What is a piece of music?   15
   3. The histories of music   25
   4. How music works   39

PART II: MUSIC IN SOCIETY
   5. How we use music   55
   6. How we learn about music   67
   7. How we talk about music   83
   8. How music talks about us   103

CONCLUSION   121

   Further resources and investigations   133
   Sources and references   137
   Index   148

INTRODUCTION

The man that hath no music in himself,
Nor is not moved with concord of sweet sounds,
Is fit for treasons, stratagems and spoils;
The motions of his spirit are dull as night
And his affections dark as Erebus.
Let no such man be trusted.[1]

Is Lorenzo (in *The Merchant of Venice*) right? He seems to be privileging a special kind of authority to music. It is part of the wholeness of the human spirit, and the person who doesn't have it is somehow incomplete. Shakespeare's Julius Caesar makes a similar remark about Cassius:

He hears no music.
Seldom he smiles, and smiles in such a sort
As if he mocked himself and scorned his spirit
That could be moved to smile at anything.
Such men as he be never at heart's ease … [2]

Caesar is in good company here. This idea that music is necessary to 'heart's ease', or mental balance, has a venerable history. In the Bible, Saul's 'heart's ease' is restored by music:

The Spirit of the Lord departed from Saul, and an evil spirit from the Lord troubled him … And it came to pass, when the evil spirit from God was upon Saul, that David took an harp, and played with his hand: so Saul was refreshed, and was well, and the evil spirit departed from him.[3]

The idea seems to be that music exercises a moral force derived from its natural properties. According to the Syrian philosopher, Iamblichus, Pythagoras thought 'the first important lesson to learn, is that which subsists through music [for it] possesses remedies of human manners and passions that are able to restore pristine harmony and faculties of the soul. Pythagoras devised musical medicines calculated to repress and cure diseases of both bodies and souls.'[4]

The power of music derived from the mathematical relationship of musical pitches which, being part of the natural order, could bring order to the human mind and allow Pythagoras to effect 'soul-adjustments' through musical performance. Music was built into the cosmos, and we could tune into it to the benefit of our souls. Pythagoras coined a word for this cosmic musical order: Harmonia.

So, music shows us how to live in harmony, with each other and with ourselves. Plato gave this idea the status of a general principle: 'Education in music and poetry is most important ... because rhythm and harmony permeate the inner part of the soul more than anything else, affecting it most strongly and bringing it grace.'[5] It is a short step for Plato's 'inner part of the soul' to take its place at the heart of creation myths. 'When I laid the foundations of the earth ... ', thunders the Old Testament God proudly, 'the morning stars sang together, and all the sons of God shouted for joy,'[6] and one of the earliest human characters in Genesis, a contemporary of Adam himself, is Jubal, 'the father of all such as handle the harp and organ'.[7] In this account, musical skills enter the human repertoire just behind tent making and just ahead of metal working.

Music, as a type and exemplar of order and harmony, enters the realm of human governance and society together with nature and religion. The moral law becomes a civil law also. The Arcadians used music to educate their children in the ways of a peaceful and orderly community (by contrast with their neighbours, the Cynaetheans, who didn't). Orpheus used music to govern not just the human mind but nature too. Minos sang the laws of Crete; the Old Testament was memorised by being sung; tribal songs encode cultural information in the same way. Boethius put the ideas of the ancient Greeks into context for his sixth-century Roman audience: 'music is related to us by nature, and it can ennoble or debase our character'.[8]

Nor is this just a Western notion. Taoist music has similar ideas about promoting harmony, particularly between the Yin and Yang tones. Confucius remarked 'if one should desire to know whether a kingdom is well governed, if its morals are good or bad, the quality of its music will furnish the answer'.[9]

Later writers, naturally enough, applied the intellectual currents of their own times to these ancient themes. John Dryden put an early-Enlightenment Christian gloss on the idea of music as part of the natural, created order:

From Harmony, from Heavenly harmony,
This Universal frame began.[10]

The early eighteenth-century poet William Collins moved beyond Dryden's cool, Augustan classicism to describe the forging of the human passions, each with its own particular style of music, part of the emerging Romantic world-view, full of storms both within and without:

> When Music, heavenly maid, was young,
> While yet in early Greece she sung,
> The Passions oft, to hear her shell,
> Throng'd around her magic cell
> Exulting, trembling, raging, fainting,
> Possest beyond the Muse's painting;
> By turns they felt the glowing mind
> Disturbed, delighted, raised, refined:
> 'Till once, 'tis said, when all were fired,
> Fill'd with fury, rapt, inspired,
> From the supporting myrtles round
> They snatch'd her instruments of sound[11]

For Byron in the early nineteenth century, this Romantic communion with nature takes us back to music as a natural archetype:

> There's music in the sighing of a reed;
> There's music in the gushing of a rill;
> There's music in all things, if men had ears;
> The earth is but the music of the spheres.[12]

Walter Scott compared the civilising influence of music on the Ancients with his beloved Medieval age, and, by analogy, his own:

> As the fabled lute of the Egyptian Memnon hailed the advent
> of the natural morning, so when the morning of Science
> dawned upon a lengthened age, the shells of the Troubadours

sounded to the impulse of its first rays ... by the delicate touches of their songs, they harmonised the feelings of a rude and illiterate age.[13]

To Scott, music is part of the 'morning of Science'.

Understandably enough, the idea of creation as a kind of grandiose piece of music-theatre did not survive into the real 'morning of Science' and the evolutionary insights of Charles Darwin. (Interestingly, however, his grandfather Erasmus Darwin believed that plants actually moved to music, responding physically in different ways to different musical styles – Mozart being the best.) For Charles Darwin, music was the peacock's tail, part of the process of display, to help sexual selection.[14]

So the twentieth century had to invent new ways of restating the universality of music for the post-Darwinian age. Some reached for transcendence, with or without a religious element – the composer Michael Tippett spoke of being, like St Augustine, 'rapt out of time into eternity' by the power of music.[15] Others found a different form of transcendence in the seemingly limitless possibilities of music as a corporate act: 'I'd Like to Teach the World to Sing (In Perfect Harmony),' sang the New Seekers in 1971.[16] Expressed in rather different ways (and for rather different reasons), this is exactly what Pythagoras was doing.

And still the eternal truths roll on. David's harp has its echo in the modern science of music therapy. Pythagoras's ideas about the fundamental division of the natural world into musical units are reflected with striking fidelity in contemporary writings about quantum physics and string theory. We are back where we started. But these are considerations for the end of this briefest of journeys: as T. S. Eliot said,

> We shall not cease from exploration
> and the end of all our exploring
> will be to arrive where we started
> and know the place for the first time.[17]

Though Eliot also, rather worryingly, has a character say 'You will understand less after I have explained it'.[18]

At the very least, we have established that music is important.

So, let's start at the beginning – what is this thing we call music?

PART I
WHAT IS MUSIC?

1

WHAT IS MUSIC?

Music is sound.

Pythagoras noticed that certain sounds have a quality – pitch – which enables us to distinguish them from each other and that this pitch is directly related to the physical properties of the object producing the sound; the size and density of an anvil struck by a hammer, the length and tension of a string. The ratios between these properties, and therefore between pitches, can be expressed mathematically.

Later generations came up with a series of technological innovations to help them describe, record and reproduce the physical characteristics of sound, including the tuning fork and the computer. Yet the basic properties and relationships remain the same – it's thanks to Pythagoras that the frets on an electric guitar are positioned as they are.

Sound is transmitted by a wave which vibrates at a certain frequency. The ratio between the frequencies of two pitches gives the distance, or interval, between them. Complex ratios tend to give rise to frequencies which interfere with each other, producing jarring or discordant combinations of sounds. Simple ratios give rise to intervals which interfere with each other less, or not at all, and sound pleasant or concordant (the ratio 2:1 produces the interval of an octave, 3:2 a fifth, 4:3 a fourth, 5:4 a major third, etc.). These concordant intervals exist not only between pitches, but also within them, so that an individual note played on a string also contains other pitches mathematically related to that note, called overtones. The intensity and quality of these overtones give different instruments much of their particular character.

Pitches can then be combined simultaneously to make chords, or one after the other to make scales. Certain adjustments are required to smooth out the differences between less closely related pitches to make a workable scale. Over many centuries, different approaches to this problem have been codified as tuning systems.

So, a naturally occurring phenomenon of frequencies and ratios needs a degree of organisation in order to turn it into music. Nature must be tamed. Our first, tentative attempt at a definition has earned itself a refinement: music is organised sound.

The next stage is to consider how we experience this thing we call music. And this involves a variety of processes, some physical, some interpretative.

Sound travels through a medium, usually the air around us, and is collected by the ear, a biological organ which converts the pressure created by sound waves into neurological impulses. Reading these impulses involves many areas of the brain, including those associated with verbal and visual stimuli, emotion and memory. Listening to music appears to use more of the brain than any one of these, which may perhaps give us a hint as to why music is often thought to reach more deeply into the human psyche than other plunderers and explorers of the soul.

Our brains then interpret the signals they have received.

The final stage is for us to describe what we think we have heard, using words. So experiencing music is a combination of physics (via biology), interpretation and description.

Of course, there is nothing to say that the brain has to read the neurological impulses created by sound waves in the way that it does. There is evidence that some blind people, for example, experience sound as colour: the area of the brain normally associated with vision is not receiving stimulus from the eye, so it adapts to read sound as a visual stimulus instead. This happens in sighted people, too, a condition known as synaesthesia. Several composers had it, usually those of a mystical and romantic bent, like Alexander Scriabin and Arthur Bliss, who wrote *A Colour Symphony* with movements called 'Purple', 'Red', 'Blue' and 'Green'. Nature has a variety of models: bats and dolphins use sound to determine distance and position, while fish use a version of hearing to read changes in water pressure.

Agreeing that there is such a thing as music means accepting that there is also such a thing as not-music: some sounds count, others don't. As Dr Johnson put it, 'all sounds are either musical, which are ever equal, or *immusical*, which are ever unequal, as the voice in speaking, and whisperings'.[19] This is where the degree of organisation comes in. Music requires a degree of organisation which the human ear can distinguish. Normally, this is provided intentionally by a person who is making music on purpose – a composer. But it certainly doesn't have to be. Music is not contingent upon deliberate human causality, and certainly not upon a musical instrument – a baby bashing a piano keyboard is not making music, whereas a blackbird singing in a tree is. Thomas Hobbes had music as one of his 'Consequences from the qualities of *animals in general*' (his italics) in his admirably clear schematic of 'The Several Subjects of Knowledge'.[20]

The boundaries between music's roots in nature and its historical emergence as a human construct are fluid and elusive, just as they are with language. Sufficient here to end with an example. Some years ago I had a blackbird living in my garden which was in the habit of announcing its arrival by singing (quite literally and accurately) this:

Either this blackbird was a keen student of the works of Ralph Vaughan Williams, or we have established that music exists in both the natural and the human realms.

Music is a science. The composer is an organiser of sound. His building blocks are scales, chords and rhythm. Organising them into coherent shapes requires a degree of repetition – if you play a musical phrase, then follow it with a completely different phrase, unrelated in key or melody, the ear will not be able to follow a logical progression between the two. They need to have elements in common. Sequences of all kinds are a fundamental part of the way all music is assembled. Our composer uses his compositional tools to make shapes and patterns in sound. Music needs clues. It is an argument traced through sound, a logical thread which the listener can follow.

This discussion needs a brief footnote: saying that music is sound leaves out one of the most important building blocks of all. Listen to the exquisite holes in the first bar of Haydn's *Oxford* Symphony, or the dramatic gaps in the opening and closing bars respectively of Beethoven's and Sibelius's Fifth symphonies, where the composers powerfully employ silence. Those gaps appear on the page as an odd little squiggle – a rest. The rest is silence, not noise. Music is organised sound, but it is also organised silence.

2

WHAT IS A PIECE
OF MUSIC?

If I said to you 'this is an apple', you would reasonably expect
me to be holding up just one thing – an apple. If I said to you
'this is Mozart's sonata for piano in G major', I could hold up
a score with the notes printed on it, or a facsimile of Mozart's
original manuscript. I could get a CD down from the shelf,
or sit down at the piano and play. All would be valid ways
of realising my statement. So which is the Mozart sonata?
At what point does a piece of music exist? And when do
the constituent parts constitute a piece? It begins to look as
if the most troublesome word in our chapter heading is 'is'.

Broadly, there are three candidates with competing
and complementary claims to be the place where a piece of
music lives and breathes and has its being: score, recording
and performance.

The Western system of musical notation is one of our
more successful achievements. Basically, the musical score
is a graph of pitch against time, with pitch calibrated on the
y axis, so that written notes move up and down the page as
pitch moves up and down, and time calibrated on the x axis,
so that notes are read from left to right in the chronologi-
cal order in which they occur. Because it is fundamentally
simple, the system has proved itself remarkably adaptable
to the needs of different kinds of music. Multiple graphs

can be put on top of each other and read at the same time, to accommodate a bigger instrument such as a piano, or several instruments playing together. The way the y axis is notated can also be adjusted: five staff-lines have become standard, because by also using the gaps between the lines this allows for the reasonably practical range of an octave-plus-a-fourth to be written without resorting to additional little local calibrations (ledger lines). But there's nothing fixed about the five-line stave: earlier music with a smaller range, such as plainsong, used four; other earlier music with a bigger range, such as music for large lutes with lots of strings, used six or seven. Percussion music, which may indicate only rhythm, not rise and fall of pitch, might use only one line on the stave, or, alternatively, use two or more lines to indicate different instruments rather than different pitches. To be sure, the system is challenged when music moves outside the basic idea of everything moving at the same speed, for example when an instrument plays in free tempo or several instruments are asked to play rhythmically independently of each other. Even here, however, the conventions of the score can usually cope, with judicious use of additional instructions or imaginative ways of cutting and pasting the score on to the page. Innovations like graphic notation never really caught on, not because they're not clever or inventive, but because they've proved to be not really necessary. Yet however adaptable, the score has clear limits. In terms of the actual music, it will always be a kind of shorthand. Things will be left out.

Partly this is a matter of convention at any given moment. Bach's players would know what his score told them, and what it didn't (where to add trills, or how to realise the harmony of a figured bass, etc.). They would know that he expected them to add those bits themselves, and know that he knew they knew when he wrote his music down. By not writing in a trill, Bach was writing in a trill.

So performers need to be aware of the conventions in play. Mozart would sometimes write out in full a couple of bars of florid piano figuration, then follow it with a couple of bars where the pianist is faced with just a single long note on the first beat of the bar. It is fairly straightforward to figure out that you are meant to continue the figuration of the first few bars, using the starting note and harmony you are given, and working out the exact sequence of notes all by yourself, with only limited input from Mozart.[21] If you don't, and instead just play what's written, your performance will have a great big hole in it (though you can buy recordings by eminently respectable Mozartians which do exactly this). This is another clear example of what the score tells you, and what it doesn't.

Here's another: go into your local music shop and you will find half a dozen printed scores of the Beatles song 'Yesterday', all different. All will contain the tune, the words and the chords, but there may well be slight differences in the way the rhythm of the tune is written out, and all make it clear that to a large extent, you are free to realise the piece as you see fit: on your own at the piano or with a guitar, in a band, or in some other way. The only version you won't find is the one the Beatles actually recorded, with a string quartet. Why? Because it's just a song. In this case the score is a lead-sheet, not a detailed transcription of a performance which actually took place, or is ever intended to. William Byrd would have recognised that approach – he did the same thing in his consort songs, which can be played or sung by various combinations of one or more singers, viols, keyboards or whatever comes to hand. An added complication is that in cases like the Beatles, the composer never actually wrote the music down at all – there is no authentic written source. This is one of the ways in which the music of the Beatles is sometimes, rightly, regarded as representing a kind of folk music. There's no authentic written source of 'Greensleeves', either.

A further limit to the score's status as a reliable record of a piece of music is that there are often different versions of what is purportedly the same piece. So which is the piece? Sometimes composers are known to have ignored their own markings. Some composers seem to have regarded markings as some sort of private in-joke, notably Schoenberg, who would occasionally write a crescendo and diminuendo on a single piano chord, which is of course physically impossible; he even began one of his pieces with the tempo marking 'a little slower'.[22]

So what is the correct way to play what's in front of us on the music stand? Some composers have been more prescriptive than others, content to leave more or less of the process to the interpreter. Sometimes, intriguingly, both approaches can be seen on the same page of music. For example, Mozart's manuscripts are usually scrupulously legible (if not always particularly neat).[23] Occasionally, however, his own copies of piano concerto movements show a difference of approach between the orchestral and the solo writing. The instrumental parts are notated with clarity and precision – the players are expected to play what the composer wanted, and need to know what it is. The piano part, on the other hand, leaves a certain amount to the performer on the day, sometimes through shorthand instructions like 'col bassi' or sometimes through the use of figured harmony, which tell the pianist to join in the orchestral 'tutti' but without saying exactly how. Sometimes the piano part is lavishly crossed out and rewritten on the score, revealing a degree of composition going on after the work was finished, probably in performance. Perhaps no two of Mozart's own performances were exactly alike.

All written music contains this element of re-creation, of improvisation, to some degree. The score is not the piece of music. If it was, the perfect score would record a piece of music perfectly. It doesn't. Music typesetting programmes notate a piece of music with digital accuracy, but if you play them back through your computer's inbuilt sound card you get something which nobody would dream of listening to. You get the music with perfect accuracy, but what you don't get is the music.

Musical twelve-year-olds in the UK pass through a coming-of-age ritual known as 'Grade V theory'. One such neophyte of my acquaintance was faced with the task of writing out in full the notes of an ornament or trill which its composer had indicated by a funny little squiggle or symbol, according to convention. 'If he wanted us to play it like that,' asked the inky young student, finding himself increasingly tied up in a tangle of demi-semis, 'why didn't he write it like that?' It's a fair question. The answer, of course, is to save himself time, effort and resources. Why should he use his paper, ink and pen, if you can do it for him more or less as he intended? But the twelve-year-old's stricture could equally be applied to all music. All written music is a kind of shorthand. The score is not the piece.

So what about a recording? The question is immediately raised – recording of what? Of a performance. And also, of course, of the work of an editor, producer, engineer, microphone designer, acoustician and/or architect of the studio or building where the recording was made, and many others. As with notation, the degree of involvement of these professionals varies with the conventions and technological reach of different periods and styles of music. Certain kinds of modern pop music are almost entirely the work of the producer. Vocals are submitted to all sorts of pitch-bending and other manipulation, so that the idea that this is an actual recording of an actual performance more or less vanishes under the beeps and swoops. The same applies to classical recordings, too. Reverb is added, balance is adjusted, takes are spliced together, infelicities edited out. It is possible to listen to recordings of duets sung by people who were never in the same room at the same time, or on the same continent, or even alive at the same time. Nat King Cole and his daughter Natalie recorded the voice parts of 'Unforgettable' forty years apart. The singer Aled Jones has issued an album of himself as a boy treble duetting with himself as an adult baritone, which has a kind of spooky, Dorian Grayish quality to it, as if we are listening to someone ageing and not ageing at the same time. Some purists don't like the intrusion of technology into the pure musical experience.

The antidote is the live recording (a curious oxymoron). Yet there's nothing wrong with tidying up a performance for repeated listening at home. There's nothing morally questionable about removing mistakes or the sound of a bus going past. The recording is an image. Listening to live music and then a recording is a bit like looking at a beautiful landscape and then at a photograph. The live experience is fuller, more immediate and more subject to change (the thrilling and the dampening), but fixing that experience into a form that will repay repeated visits in your own home requires staging, composition and editing. An image needs touching up.

So score and recording appear both to be approximations, approaching the idea of a piece of music from opposite ends (the graphic image and the sonic image). In performance, a piece may draw on both of these approximations, and on something else: a shared, learned inheritance which performer and listener both know, not written down anywhere, mixed with a fair helping of the performer's own thoughts and ideas. Unlike some other arts, music exists in time, not in space.

If music is organised sound, then a piece of music is a pre-organised musical structure. Music is something, a piece is a thing. The degree of organisation, and the degree to which that organisation is recorded, either in writing or in sound, or in a shared cultural memory of gestures, varies: yet there are always elements of both – something decided in advance, and something added on the spot. Beethoven can write a piece and ask you to play it 'mit innigster empfindung,'[24] but he has no control over how 'innig' your 'empfindung' is, nor over a host of other factors such as the sound of your piano, the size of the room it lives in, what mood you're in, how much practice you've done on the fast bit and what you had for breakfast.

The boundaries around what constitutes a discrete piece turn out to be, like much else in this book, drawn in shades of grey rather than in lines of black and white. If Chopin sits down at the piano and improvises, has he composed a piece? If Gershwin plays two of his songs segued together, has he played one piece or two? Or three? If Handel borrows much of the music for a new piece from an old piece, has he written a new piece? It doesn't really matter. Pieces of music are not biological individuals with their own, unique DNA. Bach's 'Prelude in C major' is a piece, me practising scales is not. What lies between varies. Worrying over the niceties is semantics, not music, and this book will always try and concern itself with things that matter to people who are interested in the music (and who like it).

So for a piece of music to exist we need three individuals – a composer, a performer and a listener: with the provisos that any two, or all three, may be the same person; and indeed they may not be a person at all – our blackbird is both composer and performer, his listener (presumably) another blackbird (preferably a lady). Another proviso is that the performance doesn't have to be out loud – the young Benjamin Britten used to intrigue (and probably somewhat irritate) his dorm-mates at boarding school by reading scores in bed – giving a performance, silently, to himself.[25] There are other grey areas. When the wind makes music from open cave-mouths or telephone wires, who is the composer? Who wrote the music of the spheres?

Keats thought his life and work were 'writ in water'.[26] Music is writ in air. It only exists at all by making the air wobble around a bit. When you try and pin it down to a definition or a place, it slips away. That evanescence is part of its magic.

We are now part of the way towards answering our question, but we have also established that we can only get part of the way. It doesn't matter:

> Beauty is truth, truth beauty, – that is all
> Ye know on earth, and all ye need to know.[27]

3

THE HISTORIES OF MUSIC

The baseless fabric of music presents a particular problem in trying to trace its earliest origins: paint a picture on the wall of a cave, or carve an inscription on a stone, and the image will remain more or less for ever; sing a song and it vanishes into air, into thin air, like an insubstantial pageant faded.

Contemplation of the emergence of music has engendered all sorts of theories: about its relationship with things such as evolution and language; its links with universal behaviours like the babbling of mother and baby; and the unusual human habit of walking in rhythm (animals, by and large, don't do this: humans will often subconsciously fall into step with one another). Archaeological evidence involves a good deal of necessary conjecture – it's been noted, for example, that the areas of caves most richly decorated with Neolithic paintings often have the best acoustic properties, suggesting they might have been used for some sort of music-making.[28] The same is true of some burial structures. Early written texts are full of music – in the Old Testament it is firmly placed in the context of ritual, celebration, warfare, seduction and much else. Visual artefacts such as pictures and sculptures give a clear sense of the ubiquity of recognisably modern instruments like flutes, drums and harps in the ancient world – a striking example is the pair of late Neolithic marble statues discovered on the island of Keros, which are perhaps 4,000–5,000 years old.[29] Egyptian art is likewise lavishly set to the accompaniment of music and dancing, from the days of the earliest dynasties and indeed before.

Actual musical notation appears remarkably early – the Hurrian songs, written in cuneiform on clay tablets, are around 3,400 years old. As well as the text, the source contains instructions about how to sing and accompany it, consisting of interval names and number signs.[30] Shortly after the songs were discovered in modern-day Syria in the 1950s, a tablet emerged which proved the existence of a contemporary Babylonian theory of scale and mode. As with some (much) later music, scholars have pored tirelessly over the interpretation of these disparate clues, without definitive success: there are (so far) five different realisations of the Hurrian source, all completely different. The much later Seikilos Epitaph, inscribed about 2,000 years ago, uses a system of Greek musical notation which makes the tune explicit.[31] Taken together with theoretical writings, pictorial representations and other evidence, these sources provide a good deal of evidence about the processes and purpose of music in the ancient world, if not about the music itself. Chinese thinkers and writers addressed similar questions.

Astonishingly, some of the best evidence about the very earliest music comes in the form of actual musical instruments. Flutes made of wood or bone, with or without finger holes and mouthpieces, have been found at various sites around Europe. Some date back more than 40,000 years, to the earliest arrival of anatomically modern humans in Europe.[32] A 6,000-year-old Chinese flute was found to be still playable. Its scales correspond to those of the ancient Chinese musical system.

These hints and shadows provide at best a partial, though tantalising, glimpse of what music actually sounded like in the ancient world and before. Like the flutes, these glimpses need to be handled with care. Intriguingly though, perhaps a different kind of artefact has prevented them from trembling away into silence entirely – the living, oral tradition of performance. Certain worshipping communities in the Middle East may well sing the kind of music Moses would have recognised.[33] The Jewish shofar might be the instrument the psalmist used to 'blow up the trumpet in the new moon'.[34] Some types of indigenous folk song, perhaps including the 'tonal' languages of parts of Africa, may contain echoes of prehistoric musical communication, just as some modern populations carry a small twist of Neanderthal DNA in their veins.[35]

After Christ and the Romans, the history of music begins to take on a more recognisably modern form. The familiar procession of historical periods begins its stately parade. But the history of music is not just (or even principally) the history of musical style: it's a history of ideas, of external things like war and reformation, of technology, and of society.

The first big idea to generate lots of music in Europe was Christianity. A central authority (Rome) codified a repertoire (plainsong) and disseminated it through an administrative structure (monasteries). An intellectual dispute (the East–West schism of the mid eleventh century) caused a musical divide which can still be heard today. In the West, technically skilled musicians (composers) developed musical style by expanding the reach of plainsong, adding voice parts to it, then branching out to create entirely original compositions. Already we can see that the history of music is driven not so much by the artistic imperative of composers deciding what to do next, as by forces outside their control – politics, theology and the way society chooses to organise itself. Protestant reformations shoved music in other directions – different language, different style, different audience, different performers. Technological advance in the form of printing both caused and responded to the demand for this new kind of music-making. Again, changes in musical style are inextricably involved with changes elsewhere in the human landscape.[36]

A divide becomes apparent at this period, one which will run through the entire history of music: between 'art' music made by and for trained initiates, and 'popular' music, for everyone. In the sixteenth century, an educated European householder and his family could (at least sometimes) expect to hear good music sung by disciplined professionals (monastic or secular) in church, and make their own music at home, singing and playing from printed books of madrigals, psalm settings, devotional and educational songs and instrumental pieces. This took money and training. Everybody else had folk songs, ballads, easy snatches of hymns or psalms to tunes they already knew, and the remnants of ancient semi-magical ceremonies around the parish. The two traditions might almost overlap in the music of the town waits, with good players blowing up a storm in the square or the pub. Theatre music provided a unique synthesis of contrasting traditions.

These changes show up in the development of musical style. The various phases can be identified by the appearance of technical features, and suitable names applied retrospectively: Ancient, Mediaeval, Renaissance. The Baroque, for example, is marked by (among other features) the bass line of a composition developing a different character from the other musical lines, allowing it to support a different kind of harmony and performance style. Music starts to be more definitely and identifiably in a key, and can thus be organised by moving away from the home key and then back again. Performers take on a more defined role as soloist or accompanist, and solo writing can become more elaborate, free from the need to act equally with the other musical lines. Combine these technical considerations with trends in society such as a fad for the theatre, fashionable musical gatherings in smart (and racy) venues, claques of canary-fanciers supporting rival flashy soloists, and a general enthusiasm for froth, colour and show, and you get opera, the concerto and the sonata.

The later eighteenth century brought the Enlightenment. Its ideals were balance, rationality and manners: its music the classical perfection of Mozart. Nineteenth-century thinkers accorded a special privilege to the idea of the individual creative artist, and to music in particular. Compositions got bigger, in every respect, and became more concerned with the composer's own philosophical worldview rather than an attempt to access a pre-existing ideal.

The modern era threw everything up in the air: national and stylistic boundaries were destroyed and re-written by war and migration, recording and broadcasting allowed all music to exist everywhere at the same time, and amplification allowed popular music to turn into pop. Musicians responded in different ways – some looked to their national heritage in the form of folk song; others forged new styles like jazz; some made the intellectual case for modernism; others turned old things like opera into new things like the musical; all tried to make sense of their times – pop music, perhaps, doing this better than classical.

So far, this chapter has been an attempt to look at what history is, not to tell it. Clearly, a book of this scope cannot even begin to encompass any kind of meaningful narrative history of music.

But even if it did, that history would be wrong, in the sense that all historical writing makes choices about what to leave in and what to take out. Which history? Which music? Traditional music history has tended to focus on the lives and works of the great composers, just as general history has been about kings and queens, generals and prime ministers. This works: you can trace a line from Mozart to Beethoven to Brahms, and describe the advancement of musical style by looking at technical considerations such as the ways in which these composers treated form and dissonance. Discrete stylistic phases appear, with characteristics you can learn to recognise, like the birds in your garden. This gives you a context within which to identify and understand the music you hear. What emerges is something we might call the teleological approach to history: this happened; then, as a result, that happened. It makes sense.

It also creates problems. It leaves out the vast majority of the music most people actually heard and created, including fascinating things like folk songs, hymns, dance and party music and the music of cultural ceremony and identity. It presupposes that there is such a thing as an A-list of musical masterpieces, a canon – what the scholar Lydia Goehr has called 'The Imaginary Museum of Musical Works'.[37] This in turn implies that someone has the authority to decide what goes into the museum. Who? How do they know? It also suggests that composers who have deliberately decided to write music which is less dissonant than their predecessors (Britten, for example) have put musical progress into reverse. Were they wrong to do this? Or is their music simply advancing on another front, emotional or intellectual? Another problem comes from projecting this linear approach into the future: Schoenberg believed that his new style (abandoning key in favour of a serial method of composition) was so much the inevitable consequence of what came before that we'd all be whistling twelve-tone melodies by now.[38] We're not. Critics do this too. Joseph Kerman told us back in the 1950s that it was 'scarcely to be doubted' that '*Turandot* and *Salome* will fade from the operatic scene', because he had concluded by a process of analysis that they were 'false through and through'.[39] They haven't.

A second approach to the history of music seeks to deal with this. There is no guiding spirit of progress, no watchmaker. What survives is whatever the next generation finds useful. This is musical Darwinism, the selfish semiquaver. A composer introduces an idea. If his successors find it useful, it survives. If they don't, it doesn't. Progress is made not by steady accumulation, but by chance additions to the gene pool of musical ideas – what geneticists call mutations. If Beethoven had fallen under a bus at the age of nineteen, all subsequent music would have been different. History proceeds not in an orderly and regular fashion, but in rapid and irregular bursts interspersed by periods of relative stylistic stability, the musical equivalent of what biologists call punctuated equilibrium. Music isn't so much a great river, ever-broadening, but a vast ecosystem, infinitely interdependent.

Does the history of British music in the twentieth century start with Elgar and end with Birtwistle? Or start with Marie Lloyd and end with Robbie Williams? Both. There is no such thing as 'the' history of music. There is an infinite number of histories, all going on at the same time. Looking at just one of them, however brilliant, is limiting. Trying to see music as a whole is much harder: yet the rewards are richer, far more interesting and ultimately more worthwhile.

One possible way into this impossible task is to look for characteristics which all music has in common. We could begin by making the acquaintance of a character we find strolling through every period of history like a sort of musical Don Quixote, tilting at windmills: the creative artist, the writer of music, the composer. Who is he? What does he do? What is he like?

He works hard. Any idea of sitting around among the daffodils waiting for the divine kiss, or of complete symphonies springing fully formed out of the ether, is wrong.

It takes work, and a regular routine. Most composers spend most of their time sitting at a desk – take the full score of *The Marriage of Figaro* down from the shelf, and ask yourself how long it would take you to write it out by hand, never mind compose it as well. Mozart did both.

He may very well find himself part of a 'school' of composers working together, a ready-made fraternity of friends, rivals, teachers, exemplars and colleagues. Palestrina, Purcell, Mozart and Cole Porter all did what a lot of people around them were also doing, only better.

He will need a job. Only rarely has he been paid just to compose, or at least to compose what he likes. One of his challenges is the extent to which he can match his own artistic imperatives to the changing needs and restrictions of society. The Renaissance composer was an artisan, providing something for use to a predetermined brief, like a stonemason or woodcarver. By the Classical period he had pupated into an artist, living by the bubble reputation. Later still he emerged as an ego. All this is reflected in how he made a living. It's all there in the music. Today's composer, of symphonies and stadium rock anthems alike, functions in a market, like everybody else. Rich old ladies have, to a large extent, been replaced by Ticketmaster, the Performing Right Society, the Arts Council and iTunes downloads (though not everywhere – gleaming new opera houses and concert halls in the USA will have the names of their charitable benefactors prominently on display in the foyer, in the manner of a Victorian workhouse). This isn't a bad thing. It's one of the achievements of democratic capitalism that it has managed to take over the role of supporting the arts without controlling them: the debate about exactly how it does so will, and must, continue.

Other ways of making a living haven't really changed at all. The troubadour is an eternal character, a wandering minstrel with his lute or twelve-string guitar, captivating his listeners with a unique kind of intimate directness in return for a couple of coins in the hat. Blondel and Bob Dylan are basically the same person.

He will have to be lucky. This is not just about having the time, leisure, freedom, social position and education to pursue his art, though by no means have these been a given through most of human history. His temper must also match the spirit of his times. Mozart's classicism is the perfect analogue for the enlightened Zeitgeist of educated European society of the 1780s and 1790s. What would have happened to him if he had lived into the 1830s, when those ideals found themselves stretched to breaking point? Would his style have adapted, or would he have found himself stranded, washed up, old-fashioned and out of touch, unwanted and insecure, baffled and bewildered by Beethoven and Berlioz? It happened to others. Perhaps, like Elvis Presley, dying when he did was a good career move.

Is our composer a genius? This is a nineteenth-century concept, and not always a helpful one. It can distort as well as illuminate our understanding of, say, Beethoven, if we treat every time he spat on the floor as some sort of divinely inspired gesture. Perhaps even more importantly, it certainly doesn't increase our openness to the composers around him, the foothills to his grumpy volcano – Dušek,

Clementi, Czerny and Cherubini, all good, interesting composers who don't get the attention they deserve.

Is he nice? Do you have to be nice to write nice music? To begin with, nice music isn't always nice. Music is meant to disturb and stir up as well as simply to please. If we find ourselves enjoying Bach's music for the flagellation of Christ in his Passion settings, we aren't listening.[40] Also, we have to let our genius be human from time to time. Some notable people (including Margaret Thatcher) simply refused to believe that the sainted Mozart wrote rude songs to amuse his friends.[41] Well, he did. Surely it only increases our affection for these artists to know they were prepared to use their art in such a refreshingly un-precious way. There is no contradiction with what he did when he was being serious. Purcell's catches are even ruder.

Is he like us? Of course creative people are different: what Malcolm Gladwell has called 'outliers', people who don't 'fit into our normal understanding of achievement,' and are 'beneficiaries of hidden advantages and extraordinary opportunities and cultural legacies that allow them to learn and work hard and make sense of the world in ways others cannot'.[42] This clairvoyance is not always easy to manage. A vein of introspection, even melancholia, goes with the territory – Mendelssohn was famously personable, but many intimate accounts speak of a darker side. Both are present in the music. Some, like Sibelius, took to drink: others, like Rachmaninov, to psychotherapy. This does not imply, however, that creativity is on a spectrum with mental instability. The pianist James Rhodes has written movingly about music and mental illness, suggesting that in many ways they are opposites, because 'you can throw it at the manuscript paper, not the walls'.[43] I think there is a lot of truth in that. Music is about making patterns, and patterns can provide balance, including for those who find it difficult to discern coherence in the world around them.

Different, yes; but the successful creative musician has usually been comparatively well balanced, hard-working, highly educated, clever and demanding, of himself and those around him. He might, on occasion, appear to prioritise his art above his friends and family, which doesn't always show him in a wholly attractive light. We can sometimes find ourselves admiring the music more than the man. Yet we usually forgive him.

There will be readers who have noticed, and objected, that I have referred to the historical figure of the composer as 'he'. They are right. Composition belongs to everyone, and our language should reflect that. However the fact is that in the past, he has been mostly a he. Why is this? Social norms play a part (though few women had to submit to being muzzled quite as firmly as Alma Schindler, who on marrying Gustav Mahler was forced to sign a contract undertaking not to write any more music so as not to queer the compositional pitch for her husband). But women authors faced plenty of social restrictions in the early years of the novel, which, by and large, they overcame, often through the use of pseudonyms, usually masculine. Yet the same cannot be said for composers, or at least to nothing like the same extent. Why is this?

I offer two thoughts. First, learning to write words is something you can do on your own. If you have access to a reasonable library, and (crucially) the time and leisure to wander in it, you can practise and hone the art of the author in solitary and dedicated isolation, as Jane Austen and the Brontës did. Learning to compose requires getting out there and making music, your own and other people's, every day, in choir practice, orchestra rehearsal, military band or monastery, places which were, by and large, reserved for men. Second, education. Women were taught to play (and, of course, sing), but the kind of rigorous technical instruction in composition given to Mozart, for example, would not have been on offer to his sisters and his cousins and his aunts. It is telling that the best female composers of the nineteenth century were largely miniaturists, composers of songs and short piano pieces (and also, in a number of cases, close relations of leading male musicians).

We like to think that those barriers have gone now. Certainly, some notable characters have taken some enthusiastic pot-shots at the compositional glass ceiling over the last hundred years or so. There are lots of busy professional female composers around today, in film and TV as well as the classical world. Yet the inconvenient fact remains that there has not yet been a female composer to unambiguously share the top of the world's renown with modern masters like Bartók, Stravinsky and Britten, or living figures like John Adams. Why is this? I don't know. Will it change? Assuredly it will. But it hasn't yet.

The personality type of the creative musician recurs through time. Context changes: some build up, others break down, according to the world they find themselves born into; and these phases repeat themselves as well. In many ways, however, music history proceeds not in a straight line, or in any kind of line, but round and round, like the steps of a country dance constantly making and remaking the same shapes and patterns. And the creative tensions which give rise to musical style – between the modernist and the reactionary, the unashamed populariser and the solitary worshipper at the temple of high art – these are present in every age too. Our composer has tilted at windmills, yet most of them are still standing.

4

HOW MUSIC WORKS

All music sounds a bit like something else. Some of this sonic similarity is cultural, or purely practical. A classical symphony makes the same kind of noises as another classical symphony because they were both written for the same kind of orchestra, and that decision was driven not wholly by any artistic choice on the part of the composer, but by finance, fashion and the size of the rooms they played in. Even in areas where the composer is sovereign, like writing a tune, music will always draw on a shared hinterland of generic gestures.

Recognition is part of how we experience music. The composer has to marry that recognition with the pursuit of that elusive thing, an individual, authentic musical voice. This is not just about adopting a couple of musical ideas like a corporate logo, a kind of glib branding superimposed on the music to disguise a lack of substance – but by discovering something inside that matches the composer's personality, background and world-view. It's easy to recognise, difficult to describe, even more difficult to do. It's not just about being different from everybody else, it's about being true to yourself. Good teachers knew how to bring it out (Charles Villiers Stanford, Nadia Boulanger, Frank Bridge), a talent amply evident in the work of their pupils (Ralph Vaughan Williams, Astor Piazzolla, Benjamin Britten).

Sometimes, the sounding-like-something-else can be entirely deliberate. A film can conjure up a mood by reaching for a known musical form like a march. But care is required: occasionally composers have gone a bit too far and found themselves in court accused of plagiarism.

The case for the defence involves putting this idea of creative similarity into context. First, sometimes film music sounds like other music because that's exactly what the composer was asked to do. For *Star Wars*, director George Lucas asked composer John Williams to give him a 'Korngold kind of feel about the thing'.[44] He got it: and a Holst and a Stravinsky kind of feel, too – the models are easy enough to identify.

Second, this is hardly new. Handel borrowed unapologetically from all sorts of other composers, turning their ideas into something of his own with a twist of his quill pen, just as Williams did with his fine-liner 250 years later. The point is not whether or not Williams borrowed Korngold's theme from *King's Row*, but what he did with it – that rising seventh, those rattling triplets shuttling around the beats of the bar, those stirring parallel triads: these are new. Peter Shaffer captures the process well in his play *Amadeus*, for example, when Mozart takes a dull bit of Salieri and playfully turns it into the sparkling aria 'Non più andrai' from *The Marriage of Figaro*, on the spot, giggling thoughtlessly in poor Salieri's face as he does so (arrant fiction, of course: but, as so often, encapsulating a truth).

Third, any attempt to avoid acknowledging your inheritance is both impossible and unnecessary. As Stravinsky put it, 'good composers borrow, great composers steal'.[45] He was exaggerating as usual, but he makes the point that all music has a hinterland; it all comes from somewhere.

Fourth, debates about whether one piece of music is actually pinched from another soon founder on the fact that most music is based on a common library of scales, rhythms and gestures, making it almost impossible to prove in any legalistic sense that a particular theme was taken from a specific piece, rather than from a collection of stock ideas and phrases which both share. On 13 June 2016 Led Zeppelin's Jimmy Page and Robert Plant took the stand in a Los Angeles courtroom to defend their 1970s hit 'Stairway to Heaven' against the charge that its famous opening riff was lifted from a song by another (rather less famous) band. The BBC reported that they would be deploying what it called the 'Mary Poppins defence', because the chromatically descending minor key bass-line which features in both songs also appears in Bert the chimney-sweep's cheery little number 'Chim Chim Cher-ee'. And, they could have added, in Dido's less cheery number at the end of *Dido and Aeneas* by Henry Purcell. On 22 June the jury cleared Page and Plant of plagiarism.[46]

Laying clues is necessary. Brahms was not at fault because the tune of his First Symphony sounds like the tune of Beethoven's Ninth ('any fool can see that', retorted Brahms when someone pointed it out).[47] At the same time, integrity is lessened if the device is used to manipulate the listener. Careers have been made on the strength of Percy Scholes's dictum that 'to become immediately and widely popular a melody must possess just as much difference as will confer a sense of novelty, and no more.'[48] It's a trick – you give the listener enough of the associations of a piece they already know to absolve them from having to do too much work. You make it easy for them. Borrow the gesture, and you also borrow the thought. It's clever, but bogus.

So our composer leads us through his argument by playing with our expectations. Music does this on a technical as well as a cultural level. This can be related back to the physical properties of sound. If you play the note G followed by the note D, for example, the ear will hear the D as a subdivision of the G, and will expect a return to the G. Add harmony to those fundamental tones, and you have the sense of 'pull' towards a 'tonic', or central note, on which all music in a key (known, rather inaccurately, as 'tonal' music) is based. The composer plays with that. He can do the same with music's other technical elements, too – rhythm, harmony, texture, and many others.

Here is an example in miniature:

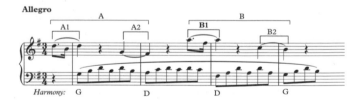

Mozart, Piano Sonata no. 5, K 283, opening.

The composer begins with a simple idea [A1]. He then answers it [A2]. The third idea is a repeat of the rhythmic and melodic shape of the first [B1]. The fourth idea repeats the second [B2]. There are relationships within and between phrases: [A1] is related to [A2], and [B1] is related to [B2]. At the same time [A1] is related to [B1], and [A2] to [B2]. [A] is also related to [B]. The composer makes patterns with keys too: [B1] is [A1] moved from the notes of a G major scale to the equivalent notes in the scale of D major; [B2] is [A2] moved the other way, from the notes of the D major scale to the G major.

There is another pattern in the spacing-out of the chord changes (which is a mirror image: G, D; D, G). Some of the patterns are subtly altered: the melody in bar 3 has a slightly bigger leap than the equivalent place in bar 1.

Things change, but stay the same. The composer sets up expectations, then plays with their fulfilment. The mind is satisfied, the ear beguiled. What looks like the simplest snatch of musical naivety turns out to conceal a detailed piece of functional engineering beneath its polished surface – Mozart is revealed as the Isambard Kingdom Brunel of sound.

There is much more to be said about these four bars. And, of course, they are only the beginning of a longer movement. This pattern of relationships and shapes is rolled out over a whole range of themes and keys. It works by achieving balance – it's impossible to say, as it might be with other music, that rhythm is to the forefront here, or melody, or key, or texture. All are in play, and all are part of the same conception, held in perfect balance with each other. It's a juggling act, a kind of magic. (And, incidentally, it also explains why bits of Mozart which look like prettified clichés on the page somehow never sound like it – a simple cadence, endlessly drawn out, seems to satisfy the structural

Composers playing with listeners' expectations by deliberately not
settling in a key: Beethoven's Symphony no 1 (op. 21) opens with a
series of ambiguous dominant sevenths; Tallis's motet 'In ieiunio et
fletu' moves swiftly from a major chord on C to the distantly related
chord of B major; Bach tells you he's about to cadence into G major,
then doesn't (Fantasia in G major, 'Pièce d'orgue', BWV 572).

needs of the moment so completely and so sublimely that nothing else will do).

Music of the classical period does this best. Mozart is the best classicist. A student remarked to me recently that he thought Mozart was a better composer than Beethoven because 'you can hear the gears grinding in Beethoven'.[49] It's a good comment.

Sometimes a composer doesn't let on what key the music is in (the opening of Beethoven's First Symphony), or sets up a key and then quickly moves far away from it (Tallis's motet 'In ieiunio et fletu', which goes from a chord of C major to a chord of B major in twelve beats), or implies that he's about to arrive back in the home key and then doesn't. (Bach loved doing this, often postponing the resolution of a cadence with a richly unexpected chromatic chord, for example at the end of the second section of the G major organ *Fantasia* – see opposite page.)

This principle does not just apply to classical music: Elton John's 'Yellow Brick Road' approaches the home key at the end of the verse, then veers off on to a totally different chord to begin the chorus, before circling back round again.

Composers do this with rhythm, too. You can't tell that the opening of Beethoven's 'Für Elise' is in 3/4, or at least not for several beats. Beethoven doesn't give you enough information. That is deliberate. A classic example is on the next page.

Haydn, String Quartet in F, op 77 no. 2, third movement (Minuet), opening.

When you listen to this (as opposed to looking at it on the page), you can't tell whether it has two crotchet beats in the bar or three, because the phrase lengths keep changing from one to the other. That ambiguity gives the music much of its character and charm. It's a game: the listeners keep tripping over their own ears. Haydn loved this sort of thing.

Later composers went further: what rhythm do you actually hear in the horn solo at the beginning of Strauss's *Till Eulenspiegel*, or the big tune at the end of Britten's *Young Person's Guide to the Orchestra*? Try writing it down by listening to it, then go and check in the score. The composer is playing with you: it all depends on setting up expectations.

This is a vastly truncated and necessarily light touch approach to aspects of musical analysis. Yet what it can reveal, or at least hint at, is the extent to which technical devices are shared by music of different types, perhaps more so than may be readily apparent. For instance, in each of the two stylistically contrasting examples on the following page, a musical structure is built from a small twist of melody endlessly repeated: turned upside down, shunted around the stave, changed from major to minor, an interval altered here or there, but always recognisably the same fragment.

The composer controls all this. So, one of the decisions he is faced with is the degree of control he wishes to exercise over his material. Musical history has given us extremes at both ends. Serial music removes from the composer some choices over, for example, which note to use next, by allocating that decision to a predetermined sequence or series. Total serialism applies this principle to every aspect of the composition. Pitch, duration, intensity, volume are all decided by a system. The composer is left with almost nothing to do.

At the other extreme, free jazz decides precisely nothing in advance. Performers walk on stage with no preconceived ideas of any kind. They just play.

As extremes often do, these opposites tend to meet at the other side of the circle. In both cases there is effectively no composer. The result is that the listener is 'baffled in performance by the absence of audible sequence or logic. The ear yearns for a structure upon which it might lean', in the typically perceptive words of the critic Donald Mitchell.[50] This is what an unsympathetic listener means when he says (about Schoenberg or heavy rock) 'that's not music': it doesn't give me the cues and clues I think I need. It is the composer's job to lay them.

Bach, Two-part invention no. 1 in C major, BWV 722 (opening), and extracts from 'They Can't Take That Away From Me' by George and Ira Gershwin. Melody constructed by repeating and transforming small units, marked with square brackets. In the Bach, the opening motif reappears more or less every half-bar in the entire piece, in various transpositions and at various pitches. Bach builds his piece by varying the pitch and key of the motif and the way it is combined with other music. Sometimes it appears upside-down, i.e., where the tune first went up it now goes down, and vice versa, marked with the bracket appearing below the notes. Gershwin uses two little motifs (marked A and B), and builds his tune partly by varying the last interval of motif A – a rising third (bar 1), falling fourth (bar 3), rising fifth (bar 5), then, when the music is repeated, the fifth is transformed into a rising sixth (bar 23). Much simpler than the Bach, but the same basic idea.

So part of what we get when we experience music is the nuts and bolts – the notes and beats. It can be illuminating to examine how we decode this information: Percy Scholes once demonstrated that people recognise 'God Save the Queen' more easily when the rhythm is played on a single note than when they hear the actual tune, with all the right intervals but the wrong rhythm.[51]

We also get memories, conscious or otherwise. We've noted that music always contains echoes of other music. It can be a measure of the strength of a composer's musical personality how confidently those echoes are assimilated.

We get cultural layers. This aspect is well illustrated when we hear a piece we know in one genre played in another – Jacques Loussier's brilliant jazzed-up Bach, for example. Cultural associations can be deliberately carried across genre boundaries for a particular effect, as when

Mahler dropped a minor-key version of 'Frère Jacques' into his First Symphony, or Jimi Hendrix strutted onto the stage at Woodstock and stunned his audience by belting out 'The Star-Spangled Banner'. This can give rise to interesting ambiguities: when you settle back on your sofa on a Saturday afternoon with 'World in Union', the unofficial anthem of world rugby, blasting out of the TV, does it occur to you that it's the same tune as Cecil Spring-Rice's fine hymn, 'I vow to thee, my country?' Do you catch the patriotic echo of Spring-Rice's words, in some subliminal way, even if you can't remember them or actually never even knew them? Are they somehow embedded, in some cultural sense, in the notes and shapes of the melody? In fact, both tunes are variants of something else, the middle section of 'Jupiter' from Holst's *Planets* suite.[52] So where does identity lie? It's like the gardener with his trusty shovel: 'it's been with me, man and boy, for forty years – it's had eight new blades and twelve new handles'. But, to him, it's still the same shovel, with all the memories of happy hours in the garden still attached.

We get personal associations. This has nothing to do with the music, but with some entirely extra-musical analogue: 'Jeremiah Clarke's Trumpet Voluntary brings a lump to my throat because I had it at my wedding'. It's the *Desert Island Discs* approach. When you hear Rachmaninov's Second Piano Concerto, do you also hear in the back of your mind the distant cough of a steam engine and the clipped tones of Trevor Howard and Celia Johnson confessing their illicit passion over the tinkling of the teacups in David Lean's *Brief Encounter*? You may wish you didn't, but (if you're of a certain vintage) I bet you do.

We experience lots of things when we experience music, and not all of them are music.

PART II
MUSIC IN SOCIETY

5

HOW WE USE MUSIC

This book divides our look at music into two – what it is, and how we use it: essentially, making and doing. It's a fake division, of course: often, making and doing are the same thing. Like so much of the discussion in this book, verbal categories are a necessary convenience, not a fact. Looking at music is not like walking through the museum looking at series of separate objects; it's more like walking round one single life-form, full of fire and light, and looking at it from different angles.

All human societies have used music. Scholars have looked for universals which reappear through time and across the world. Shared use categories include religious and shamanistic music, music for social ritual, music to control and understand the natural world (by, for example, casting spells on animals during the hunt), communication between mother and child (including the unborn), music to encode important cultural information, music for sexual selection and display, war music, dance music, and others. There are commonalities on a technical level too: some scales appear to be based on the tuning system of a culturally important instrument. Others relate to language (an area richly mined by composers such as Leoš Janáček and Ralph Vaughan Williams). Other scale patterns appear to be almost a naturally occurring phenomenon: the pentatonic

scale turns up regularly in the folk music of both the British
Isles and Japan.

Mori mo iyagaru, Bon kara saki-nya
Yuki mo chiratsuku-shi, Ko mo naku-shi

Ye banks and braes o' bon-nie Doon, how can ye bloom so fresh and fair? How

can ye chant, ye lit - tle birds, and I so wea - ry full of care.

*The pentatonic scale, found in folk music in various parts of the
world. An example from Japan ('Takeda lullaby'), and one from
Scotland ('Ye Banks and Braes').*

This field of study has evolved over the last hundred years
or so from treating the music of each culture as a separate identity, to looking at the broader question of music
in its cultural context, and from there to include distinct
sub-cultures within a tradition. An example might be
soul music: a pungent blend of African gospel, American
rock 'n' roll and English Methodism, among much else.
Watch James Brown performing as Reverend Cleophus
James in *The Blues Brothers* and you can see all three. The

field is no longer seen as existing outside the Western art tradition, but parallel with it, and part of it.

It can highlight anomalies. The relationship between the anthropologist in the field and the object of study always raises questions about where authority and the balance of power lie. Cecil Sharp collected and preserved many thousands of wonderful folk songs in England and America. Yet was he also making choices about what to collect and what kind of tradition to preserve – in a sense, creating it? When the American folklorist John Jacob Niles paid eleven-year-old Annie Morgan twenty-five cents to sing him a song in the town square in Murphy, North Carolina, in July 1933, was he summoning up the authentic voice of her cultural inheritance, or was he, by paying little Annie, encouraging her to give him more of what she thought he wanted?[53]

The lasting value of the tireless fieldwork of Sharp and his colleagues lies in preserving the folk-song repertory from changes and challenges in how we use music. This is even more the case where war and official repression play a part. The musicologist John Levy was recently commemorated as a 'hero' for contributing to the development of Korea on the anniversary of its liberation. He had recorded many of their folk songs which were then, at that time, written out of the picture, but because of his recordings, not lost. Less formal ethnomusicology can throw up interesting anomalies: an English singer staying in Tokyo went into an ice-cream parlour where the staff offer to sing to the customers. The result was puzzling – the song certainly sounded authentically pentatonic, yet also vaguely familiar: 'The Camptown Races', sung in a sort of phonetic English. A style with roots in Africa, imported to America, then again to Japan: one tune, three continents, same scale.[54]

How we use music in our daily lives is partly to do with where we meet it. Certainly not just because we have gone out and bought the ticket. Sitting and listening to music – just listening, without doing something else at the same time (dancing, praying, making love or making war), is actually a relatively new idea. Most music was not made to be used in that way. We encounter a lot of music more or less by accident, either willingly (on the radio), or less so (on someone else's radio).

Many people work to music. Others find this an inexplicable and impossible contradiction. A lot depends on the kind of work. Physical or manual effort can of course be encouraged by musical accompaniment, from the 'waulking' songs of Hebridean weavers[55] to a bricklayer's boombox. Work which involves the mind or the senses is different. Music rearranges the inside of your brain into patterns which, however agreeable, are by definition not those required for your work. People who work with numbers, or with visual images (like painters), can, it seems, sometimes keep the bits of their brain separate and listen to music without injury to their output. Music stimulates brain activity, making the processing of information faster; researchers have plotted efficiency curves of the levels at which it works best. But, bizarrely, there are apparently some people who can pull this trick while reading or writing. Presumably they can hear music and ignore it at the same time – hear but not listen. I can't. Nor is it just actual music which is the enemy: anything with rhythm or pitch, like a whining vacuum or ticking clock, sounds the knell of creativity and puts an end to the sessions of sweet silent thought.

Proper silence is hard to find. This is not the cue for a curmudgeonly condemnation of the evils of modern life: the past may actually have been a lot noisier (think of all those horses, and iron-wheeled carts and carriages).

But more than ever before, music is all around us. This is not always welcome. One writer elegantly condemns the omnipresence of music which is 'there in order not to be really there. It is a background to the business of consuming things, a surrounding nothingness on which we scribble the graffiti of our desires … '[56] Music as a background to something else is not new, from sixteenth-century church music seeking 'to draw the hearer by the ears, as it were in chains of gold, to the consideration of holy things',[57] in the words of the composer Thomas Morley, to a brass band tootling away on the prom or the entr'acte of a play. Eminently respectable composers like Telemann wrote music for precisely this purpose – 'Tafelmusik', or table music, to be played during a meal – part of their repertoire of professional skills.

So the question becomes not whether or not we agree with our complainant, but whether there is a right way and a wrong way to use music, and, if so, who decides what it is. I certainly agree with him that canned music in shops (what the novelist James Hamilton-Patterson calls 'foam rubber music')[58] can be intensely annoying. But what about a little light jazz while enjoying a summer pint by the river? The difference is one of degree, not substance.

There are lots of ways of using music. Some are more respectful of the music than others, of course: yet we must be wary of concluding that, in everyday life, some ways are by definition good, others bad. By objecting to those who seek to impose on us their preference for music in 'public houses, restaurants, hotels and elevators', our writer is doing exactly the same thing by seeking to impose his preference for silence on them. Music is bigger than that.

As well as using music ourselves, we can have music used on us. This can be for far more important, and more sinister, purposes than trying to persuade you to buy a pint or a pair of socks. Music can be used to manipulate behaviour. It can, and often has, become a proxy for politics.

Regimes have always used sacred and ceremonial music to colour in their preferred image of a ruler. On the battlefield, partisan songs have arisen naturally from the minds, mouths and marching feet of the soldiers themselves, often with more than one foot in a folk tradition – 'Lillibullero' and 'Marching through Georgia'. Napoleonic France produced many examples of this kind of song – simple verbal images carried by repeated musical gestures which lodge in the listener's brain and get stuck there, as Napoleon well knew. Historical ethnomusicology has begun to calculate the extent to which the themes and rhythms of these songs worked their way into the concert music of the time, the symphonic works of Beethoven and others.

Beethoven provides a good example of how music can powerfully express abstract, philosophical political ideas, yet be conversely less good at attaching itself to an actual political movement. His music is studded with the image of the hero struggling against his fate. This is a deeply political idea. It can be read in purely musical terms. For example, this passage in the first movement of the Violin Concerto is made up of scale figures, like so many of Beethoven's themes. It reaches up towards the higher octave like Florestan searching for the sun, the individual steps getting smaller in both melodic interval and note value, until it tips over the top and falls back a step, exhausted:

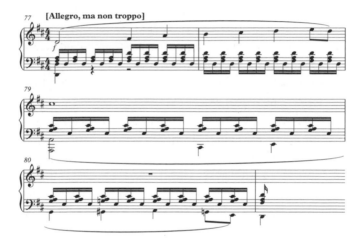

Beethoven, Violin Concerto op. 61, first movement (extract). The rising D major figure uses progressively smaller intervals: major third, minor third, tone, tone, semitone, like a climber scrambling over the crest of a hill.

The hero is trying to find his place. Elsewhere, Beethoven makes the idea explicit. The slow movement of the Piano Sonata no. 12 is headed 'marcia funebre sulla morte d'un eroe' (the only piano sonata movement he orchestrated, later played at his own funeral). He found inspiration in

tales of larger-than-life characters like Egmont and Cori-
olan. But these are abstract heroes, mythologised from
history, fiction and his own imagination. When he tried to
attach the ideal to a real political leader, it wouldn't take. The
Third Symphony was originally titled *Buonaparte*. When
Napoleon showed he had feet of all-too-human clay by
crowning himself Emperor, Beethoven furiously scribbled
out the dedication on the title page, declaring 'So he is no
more than a common mortal! Now, too, he will tread under
foot all the rights of Man, indulge only his ambition; now he
will think himself superior to all men, become a tyrant!'[59]
Political idealism of this white-hot purity is too much to be
carried by a mere politician.

As always with Beethoven, care must be taken to fillet
out the myth from the man: there are several accounts
of the changing name of the Third Symphony, though
the direction of travel remains consistent. Certainly, the
name *Emperor* was given to the Fifth Piano Concerto not
by Beethoven but by one of his publishers. *Wellington's
Victory March* is something of an exception to the principle
expounded here, but this is an oddity among Beethoven's
works in all sorts of ways, not least because it was written
to make money, conceived for an experimental mechanical
wind-band machine, and contains the tune known to us as
'For He's a Jolly Good Fellow'.

Authorities can use music as well as ban it, most obviously to promote their own ideas about themselves, and also
in a negative way. Weaponised music is not new. Retired US
Air Force Lt-Col Dan Kuehl, an expert in the sinisterly titled
field of 'psychological operations', dates the practice back to

Joshua breaking down the walls of Jericho with the blast of a trumpet: 'the noise eroded the enemy's courage ... Maybe those psychological walls were what really crumbled.' The FBI played Nancy Sinatra and sing-along-with-Mitch-Miller Christmas carols at excruciating volume to drive David Koresh and his Branch Davidian sect out of their compound in Waco, Texas, in 1993 (though Barry Manilow was apparently considered 'excessive force'). Iraqi prisoners in the second Gulf War were blasted with 'Fuck Your God' by Deicide. One detention centre on the Iraq-Syrian border became known as 'the disco'. When US President George W. Bush visited the UK in 2008, human rights lawyer Clive Stafford Smith arranged for him to be greeted with a rendition of a favourite weapon of musical torture, 'I Love You' by Barney the Purple Dinosaur. When Bournemouth City Council wanted to deter rough sleepers from using their bus station, they played Alvin and the Chipmunks on a continuous loop.[60]

Sometimes politics can engulf not just the music but also the man. Domenico Cimarosa loyally and musically supported the King of Naples until the king was overthrown by French troops, whereupon the composer pragmatically switched his allegiance to the ruling republican liberal party. When the king was restored (with the help of Nelson) Cimarosa nervously presented him with a work in his honour. The king wasn't buying it. Cimarosa was sacked (and apparently only saved from execution by the intervention of Lady Hamilton). He went on the run, and ended up hiding with some companions under the floorboards of the very theatre which had seen some of his greatest operatic triumphs. He was only driven out when one of his companions died in a fall, and the stench of his decomposing body became too much to bear.[61]

Music can heap scorn on politicians, too, from an early version of 'Greensleeves' which congratulated the Pope on becoming a father, to recent examples on YouTube. A little-sung verse of 'God Save the Queen' respectfully requests the Almighty to 'Scatter her enemies ... Confound their politics, Frustrate their knavish tricks' (or 'popish tricks' in some versions). The Sex Pistols' (rather different) 'God Save the Queen' bitterly satirizes what it sees as England's supposed self-image. Pop music has always been good at this. It's the perfect vehicle for youthful rebellion, because it's easy to shout louder than your parents.[62] But parents can probably stop worrying. Musical rebellion might become mainstream: 1950s rock'n'roll as the province of the slippers-and-cardi brigade, shuffling politely round the village hall at teatime on a Saturday. Or it might not: political protest songs by everyone from William Byrd to Bob Dylan can still sound like the howling of a wounded child. Once again, the idea of how we use music, as well as the music itself, goes round in circles as well as forward in a straight line.

When necessary, music can also code political messages under the official radar. The Reformation period saw Catholics expressing themselves in music in Protestant countries, and occasionally vice versa.[63] The logical and sinister endgame of this process is when rulers try and harness their country's music for political ends. Shostakovich reportedly described his Fifth Symphony as 'A Soviet Artist's response to just criticism', a sort of symphonic apologia for Stalinism.[64] Many people feel that the music actually presents exactly the opposite, a grotesque parody, appealing directly to the listener behind the back of official sanction and opinion. In truth, both the times and the man were probably too complex for one or other interpretation to be definitively and exclusively correct. When totalitarianism finds itself in decline, music must decide how explicit to be in response. For obvious reasons, Jewish composers found themselves in a position of particular responsibility in this respect in the decades following the Second World War. Leonard Bernstein's *Kaddish* Symphony is a rich and ambiguous statement of Jewish identity, mixing the public and the private in a poignant and personal way. Schoenberg took a more obviously programmatic approach to commemoration in *A Survivor from Warsaw*. Both pieces have received highly symbolic performances in significant locations. The Schoenberg work has been used as a prelude to Beethoven's Ninth Symphony, joining two very different prayers for peace and unity into one.[65] This idea of music as a force for political reconciliation extends to performers, too – Daniel Barenboim's West-Eastern Divan Orchestra puts talented young Israeli and Palestinian musicians alongside each other as colleagues and equals in a shared endeavour. People make music in 'The Jungle', the refugee camp outside Calais,[66] just as Britten[67] and Messiaen[68] did (in very different ways) in the European internment camps of the 1940s. Music can, must, and always will play its part in the expression of politics as an ideal, inching Beethoven and Schiller's plea ever a little closer: 'alle Menschen werden Brüder'.

Can any music be genuinely apolitical? It is one of those questions which quickly becomes circular. We've established that all music has context. The context subsists in human relationships. Politics is the word we use for how those relationships organise themselves into society. On this reading, the question is less the extent to which music is influenced by politics or vice versa, more that, fundamentally, music and politics are both about how we talk to each other. They are complementary and necessary within a society: two sides of the same thing.

The eighteenth-century Scots political theorist Andrew Fletcher of Saltoun summed it up neatly: 'if a man were permitted to make all the ballads, he need not care who should make the laws of a nation'.[69]

6

HOW WE LEARN
ABOUT MUSIC

Just as a human individual charts the evolution of the species in its progress from embryo to adult, so a single human life follows the evolutionary progress of music.

Our first encounter is probably being sung to by our mother as a baby.

Next come nursery rhymes and playground songs. This repertoire is a treasure-house. Scholars like Iona and Peter Opie have collected and curated it as Marina Warner, Cecil Sharp and others have done for its adult counterpart. Warner says 'The Opies inspired a new sensitivity to their subject, they returned an unheard, overlooked music so that it could be heard by adult ears, and they helped uncover unexpected resources for historians, as well as psychologists, among other disciplines'.[70] Of course, this tradition is challenged by the ready availability of music which children can access electronically more or less anywhere, rather than make themselves. But challenge can also bring renewal. In the end, songs are just songs.

Many musicians come from working musical families, and have thus been surrounded by the daily practice and business of music-making literally from birth. Music is part of the furniture. The family becomes the academy. John Locke was right – 'I imagine the minds of children as easily turn'd this or that way, as water it self'.[71] Certainly, the very young mind can absorb musical ideas (and much else) with an ease and fluency which the adult can only envy (I remember an extremely eminent and able colleague telling me how, in distinguished middle age and at the height of a successful and prominent public career, he decided to learn the piano, and found himself sitting, terrified, outside an exam room waiting to take Grade 3, surrounded by small children who were clearly much more relaxed about this, and much better at it, than he was.)[72] It's important to capitalise on this early, sponge-like openness to music. Most adult music lovers can easily be encouraged to recall with vivid clarity the first time they heard an orchestra, or a favourite album, or composer. It can be like a light coming on. The corollary is: don't give up. Many people drop their music as teenage interests take over. They always regret it. So don't. You don't have to reach for the stars – just hang on to whatever ability you have to just sit down and play something – anything – by just keeping your fingers and brain in working order.

We learn about music in two ways: formally, from a teacher; and the same way we learn about life, by just absorbing it as we go along. There are infinite degrees of overlap between the two, of course, and few would embody either extreme to the extent of the young Edward Elgar, who 'when he was nine or ten years old … was discovered sitting on a bank by a river with pencil and a piece of paper whereon were ruled five parallel lines. He was trying, he said, to write down what the reeds were singing'.[73] This is the ultimate in education by instinct rather than by instruction.

The rest of us achieve our knowledge of music in a variety of ways throughout our lives.

As education progresses a divide opens between those who have music lessons and those who don't. This has implications for the social and intellectual place of music as well as for its style and quality. Music, or at least formal music, becomes something for the insider. Whether or not you get to be an insider can have interesting consequences. In around 1953 the eleven-year-old Paul McCartney auditioned for a place as a chorister in Liverpool's cavernous Anglican Cathedral. He failed. Choirmaster Ronald Woan later said 'If I had taken him on, he would probably have ended up teaching music in a comprehensive school.'[74] Instead, McCartney had to find his music-making in an instinctive, untutored way, with like-minded friends he met in the park and at garden fêtes, rather than in a music lesson. The music of the Beatles shows itself once again as a type of genuine folk music, arising naturally from the culture and manner of the streets, rather than from anything learned. It is interesting, perhaps, to note that on his most recent album *New*, Paul McCartney recorded a version of a children's game he remembered playing as a young boy, full of the kind of cheerful nonsense of the schoolyard: 'Queenie Eye, Queenie Eye, who's got the ball?'

People who care about music education have worried endlessly over questions of access and elitism. These worries have been reflected in the continuing evolution of the curriculum at GCSE and A level. They are of course intimately bound up with broader political questions such as who sets the curriculum, who pays for it, and how it is evaluated. This is certainly not the place to prosecute that particular war: worth, perhaps, just picking up a couple of themes around music education at secondary level.

First; approaches to the curriculum can be character-ised as a debate between traditional pursuits like harmony and the study of scores, and more inclusive activities like free composition and pop. The key, as always, is achieving a balance. Recording a rap song can be a good way for teen-agers to access music and use it to address issues they care about (often best outside the classroom). At the same time, the purpose of studying something is to learn something of value. Everybody would be better off knowing more about a piece of Mozart than they do now. This is not elitist. Music doesn't care who's listening to it. Nor is the study of tradi-tional harmony and counterpoint – quite the reverse; these are the building-blocks of all music. We must be very cau-tious about letting them slip down the educational priority list. Apart from anything else, if students don't learn these skills, there won't be anybody to teach them – and this is already happening.

Second; technology. Computers and electronic key-boards have invaded school music departments like a horde of honking Daleks. Computer programmes are a tool, not a replacement, and students need a teacher who will tell them that. Similarly, keyboards allow you to make whole worlds of sound, quietly, through headphones, which is fine as long as we remember that music is meant to be noisy (are these children required to play their sport in total silence as well?); the sampler and synthesiser are simply offering a simulacrum of a natural sound which is made by something being hit, blown, plucked, or scraped. Where would music be without that peerless artefact of the artistic life, the school piano ('This one go plunk'[75])?

Extra-curricular subjects get squeezed when budgets are under pressure. There's no point moaning about this, it's just the way things are. If you were a head teacher faced with a choice between employing a music teacher or a maths teacher, which would you go for? Me too. Many schools do not now have a specialist music teacher. But many schools do not have a sports teacher either, despite every head and governing body being aware of the health agenda and the importance of exercise and fitness not just to physical health but to mental health, quality of learning, life chances and everything else. That agenda is built into every aspect of school policy. The school leadership which did not do this would rightly be regarded as being derelict in its duty.

The same should apply to music. Singing is good for you. Children should do it, every day. Songs which require you to fill your lungs and create a legato line, like the folk songs and nursery rhymes in Sabine Baring-Gould and Cecil Sharp's *English Folk-songs for Schools*, are better than trying to imitate the clipped, electronically enhanced vocals on 'Call Me Maybe'. This is not elitist or exclusive. Good songs are just songs, and always have been. Accompaniment should be played live, so that children can see that music is something you make yourself, with your fingers, not something pre-packaged by somebody else, somewhere else. Most schools can find someone who can play a piano (not an electronic keyboard, so the pupils can have a bash if they want to). Singing with your community in assembly, or sitting on the floor with a drumstick or beater bashing a tambourine (or the kid next to you), makes you feel better, just as taking a big gulp of fresh air does, and for many of the same reasons. Bigger, better-resourced schools should make everybody (yes, everybody) sing great, bleeding chunks of *The Creation* or *Carmina Burana*, and if that leaves no room for the audience – great, sing for yourself.

At the higher level, specialisms open up. At the conservatoire, the job of the student is easy to describe, less easy to do: you practise. At university, music becomes an academic pursuit. Scholars have found a number of absorbing ways of illuminating music through study. One is to bring fine old music back into use. It is sobering to think that the music of Monteverdi, Purcell and even Bach, did not always hold its place at the top of the world's renown by right, and had to be rescued from the historical shadows by dedicated and single-minded enthusiasts. The work continues. Hildegard of Bingen, Marin Marais, Nicholas Ludford and Heinrich Biber would barely have been names even to well-informed music lovers just a few years ago. Research and (crucially) performance has revealed them as fascinating and substantial figures. A good deal of the scholar's time is spent nosing around in libraries, dustily transcribing minims and marginalia.

But reconstructing the music is not just about copying out the notes, important though that is. A second, related element of the task is to reconstruct the social and cultural context of the music – how it fitted into people's lives, what they were thinking, what resonances the music had for them, and what else was going on around them. It's a difficult thing to do, yet without it, aspects of the music simply remain out of reach. For example: if you sit in the cramped stalls of a theatre and listen to a Handel opera all the way through, you might be forgiven for echoing the remark attributed to Stravinsky: 'too many pieces of music finish too long after the end'.[76] How many da capo arias is too many? Yet if you remember that Handel's audience wasn't really expected to sit still, and would come and go and cheer and heckle their favourite rival sopranos like the crowd at a football match, then the whole idea of going to the opera takes on a new aspect. They heard no other music during the day. You do. You know what came next: Handel's audience had not heard the music of Mozart, Mick Jagger and the theme tune to *EastEnders*. You have. Not that you can do anything about it. Thinking yourself into the mindset of a long-dead listener in a vanished concert hall is, ultimately, impossible. L. P. Hartley was right – 'The past is a foreign country. They do things differently there'.[77] But the attempt is necessary. It liberates the music. It is the job of the scholar to provide us with a road map of how to do it.

The Holy Grail of this approach has been the quest for authenticity (one of many words which can mean different things depending on where you start from). In this context it means trying to reconstruct a historically aware performance style, by assessing evidence around technical considerations like pitch, how instruments were made and played and how big an orchestra was, alongside aesthetic and artistic concerns like speed and tone quality. It can be genuinely revelatory, like Tom Birkin rolling mildewed whitewash from the medieval doom-painting on the wall of his Yorkshire church in *A Month in the Country*.[78] Some details will always remain out of reach: questions of pitch standards and the pronunciation of Latin in sixteenth-century music, for example, have to be investigated from disparate bits of evidence and supposition, and may well founder not so much on what the right answer is as on whether there is one. Modern scholar-performers are often making a choice, not solving a puzzle. It's all part of the re-creative process.

It's also about how we use the past. To what extent do we use a historical artefact to see the world through our own eyes, or through the eyes of the people who made it? This changes. Mozart added clarinets to Handel's *Messiah*. The results sound faintly ludicrous to us today, because we have taken the intellectual step of wanting to hear this music as Handel heard it.

That's actually a bold step to take. Previous generations, up to and including the Victorians, understood that the achievements of each age by definition represented an advance on the last: Mozart was only doing what Handel himself would assuredly have done if he'd had the chance. We have moved on from that. We can look the past in the eye, as an equal. There are parallels with the advent of neo-classicism in composition in the work of composers like Stravinsky – both seek to draw the past into the present – modernism and antiquarianism meet.[79]

Perhaps, though, part of the trade-off is that we may have sacrificed some of that cast-iron confidence in what our own musical age is for. If we are no longer writing music because we are certain that it represents an inevitable and necessary advance on what came before, then why are we writing music?

The authentic performance movement has been among the most important achievements of academic music, indeed of all music, of the last hundred years, because it marries serious scholarship with real music-making. Its practitioners used to be seen as mildly eccentric outsiders, oddballs who (in the words of Bill Bryson) liked 'studying the tonal qualities of sixteenth-century choral music in Lower Silesia and wearing jumpers with holes in them'.[80] Not any more. Leading conductors freely move between period ensembles and the symphony orchestra, carrying the techniques, disciplines and insights of the historically and contextually aware approach with them.

That approach can open our eyes to a lot more than just new ways of playing old music. It involves looking at more than just the notes on the page. It has been seen by some as allied with the Heritage movement – not so much the museum of musical works as the National Trust gift shop. It applies to all music, including the brand new: the Bootleg Beatles give a historically reconstructed performance in exactly the same way as a period-instrument orchestra does. At the same time, there will always be a limit to what you can do intellectually – after that you have to let the music be music. And, crucially, there is no right answer. The search for authenticity doesn't invalidate other approaches. It isn't authentic to play Bach on a modern grand piano, but it remains true that Bach has left us a legacy of music whose inner beauty and logic is revealed by an instrument which he didn't, and couldn't, know. And in doing so, he has provided pianists with a technical challenge which they simply have to master if they are serious about playing Mozart, Beethoven, Billy Mayerl or pretty much anything else. Pianists will, and must, always play Bach. Whether he would have wanted them to or not is beside the point.

We have looked briefly at what the lives of people can tell us about the music. Thinkers will also make the attempt the other way round – what the music can tell us about people's lives. Here, the caveat about the proportionate and appropriate use of evidence is even more applicable.

For example, if a hymn tune appears in an early nineteenth-century hymn book with the tune in the tenor, using the tenor clef, then the same tune pops up again fifty years later in a new book, this time with the tune in the soprano, using a treble clef, then that little detail can speak volumes about the shifting balance of power within the parish community.[81] But this only works if we look carefully, and work forwards from what people thought and saw at the time, not backwards from what we think and see today. There is a danger of reading music history from the wrong end.

The academic study of music has become known as musicology (incidentally, also the title of an album by Prince). Academic disciplines can occasionally have a somewhat tangential relationship with real life. This one can offer real illumination to the ordinary music lover through its insights not just into the notes and how they are played, but into important matters of context such as the history of reception, gender theories and alternative cultures. The illumination works best when scholarship is matched by a real enthusiasm and love of the music and a passion for sharing it. It helps if you can write. Good books can be popular, as Alex Ross has shown.

Finally, the study of music is just that – the study of the music itself; the notes, dots and squiggles. At school, students take a course in something we call Music Theory (another curiously localised use of a word – Music Theory is not a theory, it's a practice). At higher level, this becomes Analysis – taking apart the notes and phrases of a piece by Schubert or Brahms to try and work out how they fit together (as touched on very briefly with the Mozart Piano Sonata extract above). Students will then perform the trick in reverse – take a tune or theme in the style of Bach and attempt to compose or assemble a Bachian musical structure. It's a technical exercise, often given the catch-all title of Harmony and Counterpoint.

Is there a danger that all this will take the gilt off the musical gingerbread, will reduce it to mere mechanics? Was Keats right:

> Do not all charms fly
> At the mere touch of cold philosophy?...
> Philosophy will clip an Angel's wings,
> Conquer all mysteries by rule and line, …
> Unweave a rainbow … [82]

No. You certainly do not have to be able to analyse the engineering in order to experience a piece of music. It is the composer's job to use structural and technical procedures to unfold the argument in a way which the listener can follow clearly. Looking at how the piece is put together will (if it is done well) deepen your understanding, appreciation and enjoyment. It will reveal not just how good Bach is at writing counterpoint, but how every piece is good in its own, unique way. This is not unweaving the rainbow, it's polishing it to bring out its magical colours. All good composers and teachers knew that. The surviving workbooks and teaching manuals of every age, from Morley in the 1590s to Fux in the 1720s and Mozart in the 1790s and even (indeed, especially) the self-styled iconoclast Schoenberg in the 1940s, insist on a firm and remarkably unchanging grounding in the basics.[83] They are right.

This aspect has sometimes been referred to as the 'science' of music. The application of that word to music has evolved over the centuries. The medieval mind, building on Pythagoras, saw music as a way of imitating in human form the order of the cosmos and the mind of God. The 'quadrivium' of subjects for study at university consisted of arithmetic, astronomy, geometry and music.[84] John Dunstaple, England's first identifiable great composer, was (like Christopher Wren) an astronomer first, an artist second. Elizabeth I referred to 'the laudable science of music'.[85] Hobbes divided knowledge into two categories, classing music under Science, which is something you have to do, or work out, as opposed to Fact, which is something you simply discover.[86] Dr Johnson defined music as 'the science of harmonical sounds'.[87]

Later, the term came to encompass all the practical and technical aspects of music, including playing and composing, as opposed to the emotional and instinctive aspects. Dickens's Inspector Bucket draws the distinction nicely in describing his own early musical endeavours: ' "Would you believe it, governor," says Mr Bucket, struck by the coincidence, "that when I was a boy I played the fife myself? Not in a scientific way, as I expect he does, but by ear." '[88] To Irving Berlin, the 'science of music' included writing it down (which he couldn't do): 'I know nothing about music … that is, I know nothing about the science of music, which enables the work of great composers to be handed down to you and me from the minds who conceived them many years ago.'[89] Paul McCartney tried to learn to read music as an adult more than once, but gave up every time, because by that stage of his life the dots and squiggles on the page somehow 'doesn't look like music'.[90] During the twentieth century the arts and the sciences increasingly diverged into separate, specialist disciplines. Sir James Jeans attempted to assess where the relationship had got to in his classic 1937 book *Science and Music*:

> If the question is debated as to whether the music of John Sebastian Bach is superior to that of his son Philipp Emmanuel, science can bring nothing to the discussion. The question is purely one for artists, and it is quite conceivable, although perhaps rather improbable, that they may not be able to agree as to the answer. On the other hand, if the question is, whether the music of either Bach is superior to that produced by a chorus of cats singing on the roof, there will be little doubt as to the answer. The artists will all agree, and science is able to explain to a large extent why they agree … As between two pieces of music both of which give pleasure in a high degree, only the artist can decide which gives most, but the scientist can explain why some give no pleasure at all.[91]

Jeans uses his words with care: 'decide' is an artistic judgement; 'explain' is a scientific one.

Computer technology has given science in its modern sense a distinctive and welcome role in the brave new musical age. Today's composer, record producer and sound engineer have control over the mechanics of music as never before, and over making and distributing scores and parts quickly and accurately. The copyist, that eternal gnome in the mines of music, is now more or less extinct.

Music has always involved a degree of engineering. A piece has to be put together. Musical ideas have to be worked out. Within various shades of meaning, earlier generations have regarded this process as a science. They are right. Jeans is still right too, of course: composition may be one per cent inspiration and ninety-nine per cent perspiration,[92] but artistic success still depends on starting with a decent one per cent.

Of course, this idea that inspiration needs channelling through learned processes admits of exceptions and variations, like everything else. We've mentioned Irving Berlin and the Beatles, songsmiths of untutored genius. But it's telling that this kind of musician finds success in smaller forms, where the moment takes precedence over the long-range argument (the two meet most nearly in the interface between composers like Gershwin, Bernstein and Milhaud, which we'll come back to later). And anyway, not knowing what a perfect cadence is called doesn't necessarily mean you don't know what one is, or how to use it – there are plenty of cycles of fifths in Beatles songs ('It's Only Love', 'Lady Madonna'),[93] and Berlin combines melody with counter-melody with assured Bachian technique in his 'double' songs.[94] It's also true that in more collaborative forms of composing the learning can be added by someone else. The Beatles may not have been musically educated, but their producer George Martin certainly was. Much of the detail we hear on their records is his work. Similarly, some film composers write the tunes then leave the structuring of a score to assistants, like the studio of a Renaissance painter. Some composers don't necessarily always do their own orchestrations. Others shouldn't.

This chapter began as a look at how we learn about music. It has broadened into a discussion of what we learn about music, why we learn about music, and indeed whether we need to learn about music.

People can get a little defensive about the level of their musical knowledge, as if taste on its own is not enough: 'I Know It's Only Rock 'n' Roll (But I Like It)'[95] Why *only*? You don't need to have attended music appreciation classes to get something of value out of listening to it. Children react to music in the purest and most instinctive way. Stravinsky pulled his habitual trick of wrapping a truth in an exaggeration when he said 'my music is best understood by children and animals'.[96]

On the other hand, a little learning is implicit: you can't join in a song if you don't know it. Some forms of knowledge are purely practical. If you go to a performance of Tchaikovsky's *Pathétique* Symphony without reading up in the programme how many movements there are, you might end up missing the best bit or your last bus home. On a deeper level, you will get more out of the music by knowing more about it. By studying not just the notes but their history, context, meaning and place in society, you will add layers to how you think about a piece. The best kind of study will take layers away as well. The study of music is often the study of something else.

7

HOW WE TALK
ABOUT MUSIC

One of the problems with a book like this is that we can't describe music in words. If we could, we wouldn't need the music.

A result of this is that we tend to borrow words from elsewhere – we talk about the colour, form, shape and texture of music, but these are of course visual, spatial and tactile features, not aural or temporal ones. Music doesn't have texture.

It works the other way round, too. Architects talk about slowing down the rhythm of a façade, or articulating an elevation. Architecture has proved itself an excellent analogue and comparator for music over the centuries, summed up neatly by Goethe – 'architecture is frozen music'.[97]

Musicians are often ready to talk about other musicians. This usually tells us more about the speaker than it does about the subject. Benjamin Britten once said 'the best way to make me like Elgar is to listen to him after Vaughan Williams',[98] adding later, 'My struggle all the time was to develop a consciously controlled professional technique. It was a struggle away from everything Vaughan Williams seemed to stand for.'[99] It's a fair comment, and a revealing one, but it's a comment about Britten, not Vaughan Williams (who was, after all, using his own musical style to react against the generation of his teachers in exactly the same way that Britten was).

Brahms seems to have been a particular target for the pot-shots of his fellow composers: 'a talentless bastard', said Tchaikovsky[100] (it probably sounds even ruder in Russian). Britten (again) said 'it's not bad Brahms I mind, it's good Brahms I can't stand.'[101] For both men, what Brahms had to offer was not what they needed. Of course, some of these comments have a fair dollop of professional rivalry mixed in with the musical analysis: Schoenberg said of Strauss 'the expressions he uses are as banal as a cheap song,'[102] while Strauss said of Schoenberg 'he'd be better off shovelling snow than scribbling on manuscript paper'.[103] Britten's relationship with Stravinsky was marked by prickliness and jealousy. 'I liked the opera very much,' remarked Britten about *The Rake's Progress*; 'everything but the music.'[104]

Of course, sometimes quotations of this kind fall victim to a kind of deliberate, partisan-inspired form of Chinese whispers. Rossini is credited (if that's the right word) with a number of scathing remarks about Wagner, including the famous 'Wagner has some lovely moments and some terrible quarters-of-an-hour'.[105] The two men's approach to the business of music and theatre superficially seems to suggest that Rossini did indeed have little use for Wagner. Actually, Rossini's assessment was rather more nuanced and supportive than the probably apocryphal soundbite suggests. Words can conceal as well as reveal.

One of the things for which we use words is to put music into categories. This is necessary, for the library, the radio station and the record shop. You do it too, on your shelf and in your head. But putting music into named categories sets up boundaries which, when you look, are much more slippery than the fact of naming them makes them appear.

The managing editor of a leading music radio station once remarked to me 'what makes me really cross is when people don't count film music as classical music'.[106] Is he right? To begin with, he's created his own problem by categorising those types of music as different. In fact, they are not so much discrete categories as overlapping subsets. There is film music written by film composers (*Titanic*); film music written by classical composers (Britten's *Night Mail*); music written for films by classical composers and later reworked for concert use (Walton's *Henry V*); classical music used in films (*The Blue Danube* in *2001: A Space Odyssey*); and music written for the screen which draws quite deliberately on classical models (Richard Rodney Bennett's Straussian waltz for *Murder on the Orient Express*). And film music can also turn up on the concert platform. It seems that verbal categories reveal as much about what makes things the same as about what divides them. Perhaps there was no need to get cross.

Besides, the reason a radio station needs categories is to work out what music goes in which programme. So as well as creating his own problem, the radio executive has also created his own solution: if existing categories don't work, make a new one. There are plenty of examples: classic rock, rock opera, world music and the curious catch-all hybrid known as crossover. Nor is this a new phenomenon. The term dramma giocoso was a mid-eighteenth century neologism coined by the playwright Carlo Goldoni for a new kind of opera mixing the serious (dramma) with the comic (giocoso). Mozart and Rossini exploited its possibilities hungrily. Goldoni was doing something new, so he needed a new category.

The modern age has actually been quite good at shuffling musical terminologies around. The names of rival classical radio stations have themselves come to denote categories. So do composers' names: a bad bit of Beethoven is more likely to get played than a good bit of Dušek, because Beethoven is famous and Dušek isn't. Michael Haydn, brother of the more famous Josef, might be inclined to agree.

Using words to make categories has clear benefits. It also has limitations. Categorising types and styles also ascribes value to them. In *The Blues Brothers*, Jake and Ellwood stroll casually into a bar: 'What kind of music do you usually have here?' they ask the bartender politely. 'Oh, we have both kinds,' she replies, 'Country *and* Western.' [107]

Another limitation of categories is that any given style of music has internal sub-categories, fiercely guarded by their acolytes and devotees. What counts as jazz? Jazz fans don't agree. Does free jazz count? We have already considered it in terms of performance, but how do those two little words, paired so carelessly together, spark off each other? If it defines itself as jazz, then it's not free, at least not from the associations of that word. The players may not know what they are going to play when they walk on to the stage, but they know they're not going to play Brahms. Freedom, as so often, is a relative concept.

And what about the catch-all term opera? It's worth noting that many of the repertoire items of today's opera companies were not called that by their composers – they were favola in musica, semi-opera, buffo, seria, singspiel, melodrama, light opera, school opera, folk opera, operetta, and a whole range of other terms. Wagner called his pieces simply dramas. The dreaded word musical (used as a noun) comes laden with all sorts of unhelpful connotations and value judgements.

Does this matter? It matters to the extent that it can affect how we hear the music. Opera companies won't do musicals because they would cause a flutter among the canapés and candelabras, so we don't get to hear that music sung by those singers. Categories come to denote an approach, a philosophy, a world-view encompassing working practices and contracts, as well as just a style of music-making.

Of course, all this is relative. Boundaries are being eroded all the time, not least by the sheer enthusiasm for all sorts of music of potent and popular artists like Bryn Terfel. And anyway, we don't want to get rid of categories altogether, for good practical reasons – to put on an opera, you need an opera company that employs opera singers. Categories are useful, as long as we remember that what's in them is, in the end, just music. Real creativity can result when a composer deliberately writes something that doesn't fit into an existing category, from *Rhapsody in Blue* to 'Bohemian Rhapsody'.

Verbal categories are important and necessary, but only if we remember three things: first, that the fact of naming something can cause us to define the thing named, rather than the other way round; second, that we name categories of music only after they exist (Bach didn't know he was writing Baroque music, he thought he was just writing music); and, third, that categories are useful as long as we remember that the boundaries between them are, to a large extent, shades of overlap, not fixed lines. The principal hobby of the composer Gerald Finzi was cultivating apples in his English country garden. Like Finzi's apples, musical categories reveal a good deal of cross-pollination. They are, to a certain extent, not so much apples and pears as different varieties of apple. We can enjoy the Pink Lady more if we catch the distant blush of Orange Pippin on her damask cheek.

Our use of verbal opposites is another area in which the way we use words can affect how we think. What is the opposite of classical? Pop? Or Romantic? The answer is both. Classical is one of those words which can mean different things depending on what it is being compared to. (So is anthem, which can mean a sacred choral piece, or any pop song lasting more than about three-and-a-bit minutes, depending on your age, background and what you do at the weekend.)

Classical has a whole range of different meanings across a variety of fields – classical civilisation, classical literature, classical architecture and classical music all happened in different places and at different times, sometimes whole millennia apart.

But in all its incarnations, the word classical has something in common – an implied connection to a sense of balance, order and proportion – manners, if you like – based on certain aesthetic and cultural preoccupations of the ancient Greeks and Romans. Its opposites can therefore include the pre-classical (barbaric, primitive, etc.); the unclassical (Baroque, Rococo); the post-classical (Romantic, modernist); and the not-classical (pop).

It's a good word. We know what classical music is, as long as we remember that in this context the word 'is' doesn't have any intrinsic meaning – it refers to a convention, not a fact. The same applies to the term pop music. Pop started out as a contraction of popular, but has come to mean something distinct, and different. Not all popular music is pop, and not all pop music is popular. Like all writers, I will continue to talk about classical and pop with all my carefully acquired prejudices and assumptions on display, and hope you know what I mean. If you don't, you'll have to guess. As descriptors, they are probably as good as it's going to get.

So we choose our musical opposites with a necessary degree of licence. Actually, the opposite of popular is unpopular, but it's unlikely that your local record shop will have a section marked 'Unpopular Music'. It's the same with another matching pair, live and recorded music – the opposite of live is dead.

Thinking about how we use words to describe music leads to the much-pondered question of what music means. The idea has a long history. It raises the question of whether there are certain features which are intrinsic to meaning (minor = sad, major = happy), or whether these are entirely cultural constructs. Some features of meaning are descriptive and thus relatively straightforward both to do and to hear – it is easy enough to summon up nature in music, from birdcalls in madrigals, and in pieces by Delius, Rautavaara and Stornoway[108] to storms in Vivaldi, Beethoven, Verdi and Britten.[109] Where a particular instrument has a well-established role outside the orchestra, it gives the composer a neat shortcut to conjure up that association – horns for hunting, snare-drums for marching, pipes for little shepherd boys. What varies over time is the psychological import that the composer gives to these sonic pictures: the meaning, if you like.

Ideas about meaning in music evolved alongside ideas about what music is for.

Before the Enlightenment, most Western art music evoked some sort of pre-existing psychological state, like a humour, or a type. This could be human: a happy lover sings 'Fa-la-la', a sad one 'Ay, me!' More often the humour was some aspect of the divine. Archbishop Matthew Parker made this explicit in his description of the various characters of a set of psalm tunes by Thomas Tallis:

> The first is meek, devout to see,
> The second, sad, in majesty,
> The third doth rage, and roughly brayeth,
> The fourth doth fawn, and flattery playeth … [110]

Music of a middling, neutral character was described as 'indifferent' or 'mediocre'. The Baroque period came up with the notion of 'affects', musical gestures which carried a ready-made emotional import – the 'dying fall' for a lover's sigh, trumpety rhythms for revenge or war. Odes addressed by Purcell, Handel and others to the patron saint of music, Cecilia, make this explicit. The library of musical gestures becomes like the cast of a play, every man in his humour. The nascent Romantic movement allowed artists like Goethe to start describing his (or his character's) own, individual reaction to things, rather than borrowing a stock response. Nature provided a particular trigger for investigating an individual's place in creation and the meaning of his existence. Mendelssohn's *Hebrides* Overture is no more a simple evocation of wind and waves than J. M. W. Turner's stormy seascapes, but the awestruck response of a human individual, humbled into trying to work out his own place in the natural order.

A further stage is for the listener to find their own personal meaning in music. For the hymn writer Charles Wesley, a demure verse anthem by William Crotch, 'Out of the Deep', provided the trigger that ignited his new, highly emotional take on Christianity – nothing to do with Crotch's own, modest religious sentiments.[111] Alex and his 'droogs' in Anthony Burgess's *A Clockwork Orange,* and the fearsome Colonel Kilgore of the 1/9th Air Cavalry raining fire from his helicopter gunship in Francis Ford Coppola's *Apocalypse Now*, pumped themselves up to commit the most appalling ultra-violence partly by listening to Beethoven and Wagner. Is that what that music means? It's the meaning those men found in it. More pacifically, in his novel *A la recherche du temps perdu* Marcel Proust allows his main character to discover a whole world of meaning in a little phrase from a violin sonata, certainly more than its composer Vinteuil (based on the real figure of Saint-Saëns) intended or realised was there.[112] The androgynous figure of Proust provides a neat entrée to one of the most vexed areas of the search for meaning in music – whether it contains elements that can be distinguished as distinctively masculine and feminine.

One place where this dichotomy has been identified is within the musical structure, much evident in classical music, known as sonata, or first movement, form. Bluntly, this works by presenting two contrasting themes, one after the other, and then working out the relationship between them in a form of musical discussion or dialectic, leading to a modified reprise of both. Many writers have characterised this process as ascribing masculine features to the first theme (which is in the home key and might, typically, be louder and more assertive) and feminine to the second (which is in a secondary key and may be more lyrical in character).[113] Some have gone further – asserting that where both themes are reprised in the home key (the key of the original first theme) this represents the feminine being forcibly subjected to the dominance of the masculine, providing a psychological analogue for a century-and-more's worth of gender inequality and oppression.

This is, of course, a vastly simplistic account both of sonata form and of one (among many) interpretations of it. It does, however, perhaps provide a way into the idea of a particular kind of meaning in music; and, perhaps more usefully, a way out. For a start, it only works if you choose examples which fit the theory. Not all pieces in sonata form have a 'masculine' first theme and a 'feminine' second: some present their themes the other way round. Many such movements don't reprise both themes in the home key as the theory suggests they should. Perhaps most importantly, composers were (as always) not working to a pre-existing model, but were experimenting with balance, structure and the whole idea of how to move away from and back to a set of opening ideas. The ways in which they did this were infinitely fluid and varied. They weren't following the rule book but writing it. The best chronicler of these matters, Charles

Rosen, puts it like this: sonata form is 'a feeling for proportion, direction, and texture rather than a pattern'.[114] Trying to read a particular meaning into a particular musical structure will, it seems, only ever be partially, and selectively, successful.

Some writers have gone further: certain chords and combinations of chords reveal not just masculine and feminine features, but specific aspects of a composer's nature, including, under certain circumstances, an identifiably gay part of his or her personality. The argument broadens into a consideration of gendered theories of history, performance and interpretation.[115]

None of that is the music's fault. Great composers have reflected the range and fluidity of the human condition in their own way. Trying to pin their insights down into false dichotomies like gay and straight, masculine and feminine, is not so much wrong as limiting, and therefore, ultimately, not very interesting.

A further stage of thinking about meaning in music is considering whether certain musical gestures can be associated with certain verbal or emotional equivalents: does the interval of a third mean something different from a sixth, something we can identify, categorise and describe? This idea was explored by Deryck Cooke in his 1959 book *The Language of Music*.[116] It's a fascinating argument, particularly in the way it traces how certain phrases and gestures have moved through time. But many will feel that the idea of a musical 'dictionary' remains unconvincing. Cooke himself saw the exercise as more of a 'phrase book' of musical meaning.

Another important writer, Theodor Adorno, addressed the question not just of whether a particular chord has meaning, but whether it has an intrinsic value, and whether this changes over time with the way it is used. His example is the diminished seventh chord, composed of three minor thirds on top of each other:

On its own, the chord is unstable in terms of key. Baroque composers would typically exploit this quality in order to reinforce a sense of key by using it to delay a return to a home key:

Bach uses several diminished seventh chords in the peroration of the Prelude in D major from Book 1 of Das wohltemperierte Klavier *(BWV 850) to prepare, delay and reinforce the eventual return to the home key (middle of bar 30 to end of bar 31, bar 33 beat 1, bar 34 beats 1 and 2).*

Into the nineteenth century, the ambiguities of the chord allowed composers to slip sideways into unexpected keys:

*Two extracts from the first movement of Beethoven's Piano
Sonata No. 8 in C minor, op. 13, known as Sonata* Pathétique.
*The diminished seventh chord on the third beat of bar 3 is the same
as the chord on the third beat of 135, but one is used to lead to
E flat major, the other to E minor. The composer is exploiting the
harmonic ambiguity of the chord.*

Later, the chord became a gesture in its own right, divorced from its place in a longer range key structure:

This composer isn't.

Adorno regarded this change of use as an audible cheapening which rendered the chord itself valueless to the point of being unusable: 'for the technically trained ear, such vague discomfort is transformed into a prohibitive canon'. The 'chord itself', not just the way it is used, has become an 'obsolete form ... even the more insensitive ear detects the shabbiness and exhaustion of the diminished seventh chord'.[117]

Leaving aside Adorno's rather patronising distinction between the 'trained ear' and the 'insensitive ear', has he proved that 'the chord itself' has irrevocably lost all capacity for saying something worth hearing?

I don't think so. The next example is a parallel case, taking two instances of the use of another kind of seventh, the dominant seventh. The first lets the dominant seventh lead to a tonic, as functional classical harmony says it should. The second doesn't. The expectation that it should do so turns out not to be inherent in the chord after all. That expectation is not so much confounded as simply removed. Debussy has rearranged our brain: and there are lots of other ways of dealing with this chord between and beyond these two.

Two examples of another kind of seventh, the dominant seventh: 'Der Dichter Spricht' from Kinderszenen, op. 15, *by Schumann (dominant seventh chords on the first beats of bars 1 and 2), and 'La fille aux cheveux de lin', no. 8 from Book 1 of the* Préludes *by Debussy (dominant sevenths at bar 8 beats 1 and 3, and bar 9 beats 1 and 2).*

Anyone who has sung in a moderately ambitious choir knows that if you spend time sight-reading a contemporary piece by Jonathan Harvey or James MacMillan, then turn back to Palestrina, the fourths and fifths in the Renaissance music don't make quite as much sense as they did before, at least until you get used to them again. Go back even further, to medieval music, and expectations change again. Chords and intervals have context. Meaning, like so much else, is fluid. It is perfectly conceivable that a composer will devise a musical language which can present the diminished seventh in a new and convincing way. By the same token, plenty of composers have found ways of assimilating the language of older music into their own world-view. Reports of the death of the diminished seventh have probably been exaggerated.

The twentieth century approached the question of what music means from other directions as well. Two causes celèbres will stand as examples. In 1952 the American experimentalist John Cage composed a piece he called *4'33"*, which consists entirely of silence. The ambient sounds of the room where the performance is taking place become the music. In 1969 Alvin Lucier composed *I Am Sitting in a Room*, in which he recites a short text describing what he is doing, recording it at the same time, then plays back the recording while reciting the text again and records both, then plays that recording back while reciting the text for a third time, and so on until the multiple recitations blur into and cancel each other out. Verbal meaning vanishes, and all that is left is sound. These pieces represent music as philosophy more than music as music. As well as their broodings on the nature of sound, they seem to contain within themselves the implication that the quest for ever greater modernity is over. We are, with Francis Fukuyama, at 'the end of history'.[118] A conservative reading of what classical music did next might be seen as confirming this. In any event, these thought-experiments certainly challenge our opening ideas about music as 'organised sound': just as well, then, that I played my get-out-of-jail-free card early on, by characterising that definition as having boundaries of more or less infinite fluidity.

The search for meaning in music is elusive. That doesn't mean it's wrong. The music of Elgar often has a yearning, restless, unsettled quality. Can we hear in that quality an echo of his own insecurities, social, financial, educational, religious and personal? If we want to, yes. If you really feel like it, you can hear 'repressed homosexual panic' in Beethoven, as one writer claims to (I don't).[119]

The discussion circles back to the problem with which this chapter began: the only medium we have to describe meaning in music is words; and words and music do different things. The composer Aaron Copland put it like this: 'Is there a meaning to music? – My answer to that would be "Yes". Can you state in so many words what the meaning is? – My answer to that would be "No". Therein lies the difficulty.'[120]

The attempt to solve that difficulty is hinted at in the title of the Cooke book mentioned above. Is music a language? Many people have been led to ask that question. Others have turned it round and asked, is language a music?[121]

It is actually quite a good example of the category problem: the question only makes sense if we start from the position that these are identifiably separate and distinct entities, which can thus be compared and contrasted.

Are they?

Of course, there are things that one can do that the other can't. Music is not a language for conveying precise verbal information. You can't write your tax return in music. But, as with other categories, there are areas of overlap. You could, for example, quite easily devise a way of using musical gestures to give someone directions: rising pitch means turn left, falling pitch turn right, etc. Nature uses music this way.

Approaching the question via the other category, it appears that language, the medium of precise verbal communication, therefore has less need of musical features like pitch and rhythm. This is true: but, again, only up to a point. Human society has plenty of examples of 'tonal' languages, where a syllable which has the same basic pronunciation can mean two or more completely different things depending on how it is inflected in speech. Here's an example. The Mandarin words for hemp, mother, scold, and horse are all pronounced 'ma'.[122] The difference in meaning is conveyed by vocal pitch – how high it is, whether it stays the same, rises, falls, or both: music. Westerners fondly imagine that we don't do this. To the English, however you pronounce it, a kiss is still a kiss.

Actually, in a limited way, we do. There is a curious category of pairs of words in English which share the same spelling and basic pronunciation but mean something different depending on where the stress falls. Often these are verb/noun pairs, sometimes related in meaning, sometimes less so. Examples are process/process and permit/permit, which mean different things depending on whether the first or second syllable is stressed. Word-stress is a function of rhythm: music.

And, of course, aside from the literal, there are whole worlds of meaning and interpretation in the way the wonderful liturgy of the English language is performed. It's not difficult to catch the moment at which actors and orators like Richard Burton and Martin Luther King cross the line into singing.

So the categories of music and language are different but overlapping: parts of a spectrum rather than separate entities. The commonalities have led some thinkers to look at the possibility of a common origin: what the evolutionary musicologist Steven Brown has called the 'musilanguage'.[123] It's a neat formulation which can remind us of what unites the two forms of communication rather than divides: and not, perhaps, only in the distant evolutionary past.

The question of whether music is a language quickly becomes circular, like one of those Celtic serpents twisted in bronze, eternally chasing its own tail. We set out to prove the two things are the same by first of all assuming that they are different. It's not really anything to do with music. It's a sort of verbal sleight-of-hand, as when the Bonzo Dog Doo-Dah Band asked 'Can Blue Men Sing the Whites?'[124]

We need to stop worrying. This book, like all writing on the subject, is a tiny testament to the twin facts that we can't describe music in words, and that we can only describe music in words. Words become part of the act of interpreting the music. Used well, they become part of celebrating it too.

8

HOW MUSIC TALKS ABOUT US

Despite the overlaps and the limitations of verbal categories, it's clear that music does come in types, and that the types don't just contain notes but people too. Fans attending a jazz gig look, dress and behave differently from punters at a rock concert, or the audience at a string quartet recital. Your music says something about you.

The problem with this is that tribes emphasise division at the expense of commonality. Duke Ellington said this about his own field of music: 'jazz is the man you wouldn't want your daughter to know'.[125] It's an instructive remark. He characterises music as a person, and seems to be speaking to a worried father, an older man, responsible for a perhaps impressionable young woman. Watch out – jazz is different.

It's sometimes possible to think that he's right. People who enjoy different kinds of music look at life differently. The differences can be apparent if you ever have to get jazz and classical musicians together at the same time. Working practices and the shape of the day don't necessarily match. Time itself means something different. It's there in the music – a classical piece observes a clear, well-ordered, preordained structure, like the performer's day: the jazz piece, by contrast, can just go on for as long as it needs to.

All music has its groupies. Signing up is a sign of who you are. It's also to do with the curious thing we call taste, which is itself a function of personality. Some people find the cerebral logic of a Purcell viol fantasia endlessly absorbing. Other music seems to demand a more emotional response, like the loud cheering which greets a good performance of, say, a symphony by Mahler. This doesn't often happen at viol recitals. The Purcell fan and fantasia fancier, who has probably never felt the urge to cheer during a concert, may wonder what the music of Mahler has to offer him. The behaviour of the crowd at a rock concert may appear even more alien.

Does this matter? It matters because joining one tribe can make you instinctively fear and mistrust the other. So their music remains out of reach. You can end up missing out on things you might enjoy. Good music will remain undiscovered. This is a shame. Ellington also said: 'There are simply two kinds of music, good music and the other kind.'[126]

As well as summing up types of people, music can sum up periods and places too. An earlier chapter touched on how a successful composer's manner matches the spirit of his times. The analogue can be made to work the other way round. Asked to evoke the atmosphere of, say, fashionable mid-eighteenth-century London, the musical director of a play or a film might well reach for some suitably jaunty bit of Handel. For a Jane Austen costume drama, a genteel snatch of Haydn (or skilful parody, such as Carl Davis's period-instrument theme for the BBC's *Pride and Prejudice*). Edwardian imperialism equals Elgar.

What about after that? These examples all come from the classical side of the tracks. What about the twentieth century? How would you summon up the swirl and bustle of 1930s New York? Classical music is much less the obvious go-to: Copland's *Quiet City*, possibly, but much more likely the music of Gershwin (think of the opening of Woody Allen's *Manhattan* and that great wailing clarinet from *Rhapsody in Blue*, like the soulful sighing of a thousand police sirens). Repeat the exercise for England in the 1950s, or 1960s, or 1970s, and classical music has completely lost its ability to do this: your musical analogue for the era is rock, the Beatles and disco. This is one of the ways in which the splintering of musical style in the modern era mirrors the fracturing of society and artistic movements. Types become more polarised. Michael Tippett called his autobiography *Those Twentieth Century Blues*. No longer was the composer presented with a ready-made style to inherit and develop in his own way. Instead he was faced with a sort of DIY schizophrenia. Tippett knew that.

The links between certain types of personality and particular approaches to music became easier to see during the twentieth century. But the modern age certainly didn't invent the phenomenon. The personality types recur through time. So does creative conflict between them.

One pair of opposites which keeps turning up through musical history is the reactionary and the modernist. One looks back, the other forward. One seeks to build up, the other to break down. One attempts to perfect the language and manner he inherited without fundamentally changing it, the other to destroy it and start again.

Pairs of composers who articulate these two approaches can often be found as near contemporaries: Palestrina and

Monteverdi; Mozart and Beethoven; Brahms and Wagner; Strauss and Schoenberg; Britten and Boulez. For obvious reasons, the pairings often appear at the cusp between periods of stylistic history – the punctuations in the punctuated equilibrium, to return to the language of evolutionary biology. Sometimes you can see both types in the work of a single composer – at opposite ends of the seventeenth century the music of both Monteverdi and Purcell moves between old-fashioned, learned Renaissance-style counterpoint and Baroque harmonies and gestures, sometimes in the course of a single piece.[127] But it was in the twentieth century that the question became a vital matter of integrity. Style became a matter of political correctness. You were a card-carrying modernist, or you were a hopeless, lazy reactionary. And like all such movements, the key to acceptance was who decides who's up, who's down, who leads and who is led. When William Glock headed the music department at the BBC in the 1960s, whole careers, indeed whole schools of composition, flourished and fell like ancient empires at his whim. Composers themselves could be viscerally intolerant if they felt a colleague had stepped off the one true path, as is shown in the exchanges between Luigi Nono and Karlheinz Stockhausen about Nono's pieces for the avant-garde festivals held at Darmstadt in the 1950s.[128]

The problem with the concept of the avant-garde is that it presupposes that there is a garde for you to be avant: I'm ahead of you, which, by definition, also means you're behind me. Being modern becomes the point. Bartók asked a fellow composer 'Mr Nielsen, do you think my music is modern enough?'[129] Messiaen excoriated lazy, backward-looking composers, 'les artisans du sous-Fauré, du sous-Ravel. Paresseux, les maniaques de faux Couperin ... '[130] The good opinion of the listener becomes irrelevant: Harrison Birtwisle said 'I can't be concerned about my audience. I'm not running a restaurant.'[131] The purest expression of this view was the Society for the Private Performance of Music, set up by Schoenberg and others in Vienna in 1918, which kept the audience out. There were no listeners. None were admitted. The musicians were, quite literally, talking to themselves.

Bartók and Messiaen, and, in a different way, Schoenberg, used this approach to create music which demands and commands the continuing attention of the world. But not everyone is Bartók. Today's would-be Birtwisles, serving up their modernisms in some thinly attended late-night contemporary music seminar, might content themselves with the reflection that they're not running a restaurant, but they might end up cooking for one.

The opposite approach is to 'find out what your audience wants, and give them that', in the words of Irving Berlin.[132] This concept would have been entirely acceptable to serious composers of the past, including Mozart and Handel, and certainly Verdi and Puccini.

The residue of this division is that classical concert programmers today have to put new music alongside familiar classics in order to get non-specialist audiences to come and hear it. It used to be the other way round. If Mendelssohn wanted to introduce people to the music of Bach, he had to tempt them in with a new piece of his own.

Of course, treating modernists vs. crowd-pleasers as a

binary division vastly oversimplifies a complex spectrum of music of all types. Like Monteverdi, some recent composers have been both: the late, great Peter Maxwell Davies spent the early part of his career as the ultimate wild child of contemporary music, blaspheming and demolishing his way through every convention he could find. He also wrote tuneful folky pieces and lots of music for children. Of course, he was criticised for stylistic polyglotism, and his response would be delivered in that cheeky, childlike, but uncompromisingly honest and direct way of his, with just a hint of mock shock: 'I've been called a prostitute – well, fine. In that case, so was Mozart.'[133]

It's about being true to yourself. Some people are modernists, some are not. So, what is modernism? To begin with, it appears to have little to do with being modern. The shock of the new has nothing to do with being new. Among the music which classical audiences routinely find most challenging and modernist today is the music of Schoenberg, written a century and more ago.

Also there is an idea, perhaps dating back to Beethoven, that the modernist composer is somehow ahead of the rest of us, that patience is a virtue and we'll catch up in the end, so that what on one day sounds advanced and challenging won't once we get used to it. Not always. When Beethoven's musicians first played through his revelatory, revolutionary late string quartet in A minor, they told him 'that's not music', so he made them play it again in order to try and comprehend the fullness of his visionary, modernist statement. We're still trying.

Modernism is something to do with shaking up

expectations. Not everyone wants their expectations shaken up. Philip Larkin said 'It seems to me undeniable that up to this century [the twentieth] ... music was an affair of nice noises rather than nasty ones. The innovation of modernism in the arts consisted of doing the opposite. I don't know why.' Larkin aimed his ire at a particular kind of iconoclastic modernist: 'Charlie Parker wrecked jazz by – or so they tell me – using the chromatic rather than the diatonic scale. The diatonic scale is what you use if you want to write a national anthem, or a love song, or a lullaby. The chromatic scale is what you use to give the effect of drinking a quinine martini and having an enema simultaneously.'[134] Fascinatingly, Larkin's criticisms of Parker are strikingly similar to those sometimes levelled at Schoenberg – the musical line is so chromatic that the listener can't tell how, or indeed whether, it fits with what's going on around it. On at least one occasion, we are told with a mocking sneer, a player in an ensemble picked up the wrong instrument by mistake and thus played his part in a Schoenberg piece a semitone out all the way through. Nobody noticed. Much derision follows. Charles Rosen mounts a fascinating defence against this charge: because the composer has liberated the line from a sense of key, its exact relation to the harmony of the rest of the ensemble is no longer the point, or at least much less the point. The line has a logic of its own.[135] It's a partial defence at best, and not completely convincing. But it makes an intriguing point. Certainly, you could take certain solo passages by Parker or other jazz musicians and play them, say, a minor third higher while keeping the backing the same. It would still make sense

– just a different kind of sense. Modernism means adjusting what we think we are entitled to expect to hear – listening differently as well as writing differently.

Schoenberg said 'my music is not modern, it is only badly played'.[136] Modernism is a function of attitude and personality, of your take on history and of your view of the nature of progress. How we look at existing music is, in a way, a sort of predictive pre-echo of how we think the future is going to look at us. In 1924, bandleader Paul Whiteman thought that the idea of putting Elgar alongside a new concert jazz work presented such a novel challenge to his audience that he called the concert 'An experiment in modern music'. The new piece was *Rhapsody in Blue* by George Gershwin. It would be perfectly justifiable today to take Whiteman's title and use it as the strapline for a concert consisting of music by, among others, Gesualdo, Miles Davis, Beethoven and The Clash.

Our music can speak volumes about us, our world, and the way those two things fit together. We choose our music in the same way that we choose our friends, our interests and our politics, and for the same reasons – because it mirrors who we are.

What is there to choose from? What's on the menu? If music does come in types, and those types in turn reflect different kinds of people and philosophy, does it follow that some types are better than others? Can some styles reach further than others? If so, how? Simplistic divisions like pop and classical at least have the benefit of clarity. We can compare their technical features and qualitative capabilities because it's easy to tell which is which.

Is it? How?

First, technical differences. One element which can be analysed and described is the way a tune is accompanied. This becomes readily apparent when the same tune appears in both genres. The song 'A Groovy Kind of Love' (recorded by Phil Collins, among others) uses the tune of a gracious kind of rondo by Clementi.[137] One sounds like a pop song, the other like an early nineteenth-century piano piece, yet the music is the same. The clues (or 'tells', as behaviourists call them) which we use to distinguish one style from another can, as with people, be largely about how they dress.

Another observable difference lies in performance style. This is not just about sound but about how both performers and listeners behave. What would happen if the audience at a Green Day concert sat politely in silence and applauded at the end of each piece? Actually, the question works the other way round – if that's what they thought their audience was going to do, they wouldn't write their music like that. Music is a conversation between two parties, and like a real conversation it requires the expected reactions from the party who is not speaking.

Performance style is fluid. So is cultural acceptance. A minor flappette could be observed developing over South Kensington a decade or so ago when the music of the Beatles was finally first performed at the Proms, albeit in suitably dinner-jacketed and impeccably Anglicanised arrangements by the estimable Kings Singers. Sir Henry Wood would have raised a sculpted eyebrow in disapproving surprise. This isn't just about modern pop music, either: ballads, part-songs and the cries of town waits were all once the music of the street and the informal knees-up in the pub. All will now be found tucked away in the dustiest corner of the specialist radio schedule and scholarly archive. Pop music can become classical – and occasionally, vice versa.

There are also differences in the way the music is composed. Generally, pop music and its subsets are created more collaboratively than is classical. In the works of Lennon and McCartney, not even Lennon and McCartney could always have told you for certain which bits are Lennon and which McCartney. They did it together.[138] Many pop songs list multiple writers – the song is crafted in the rehearsal room and recording studio, with contributions from band members, producers, arrangers and many others, as well as just the person who had the original idea. Musical theatre pieces are likewise often knocked into shape via a collaborative process, partly because they involve so many different areas of expertise. With *Guys and Dolls* Frank Loesser's songs came first, then producers Cy Feuer and Ernest Martin had the idea of getting first Jo Swerling and then Abe Burrows to fashion a book based on stories by Damon Runyon around the songs. It's not the way the textbooks tell you to write a coherent piece of music theatre, but it worked brilliantly. Classical music, by contrast, tends to represent the unsullied vision of a single mind. It has to. You can't write a symphony by committee (occasional attempts at multi-composer pieces sometimes founder on a lack of overall coherence and, perhaps counter-intuitively, can end up sounding too much the same). But a composer like Tippett, for example, might occasionally have benefited from the attentions of a really good editor or collaborator, not so much for the music itself, which is always fresh and engaging, as for his forays into some less than convincing subject matter. Taking advice is an important skill.

At the analytical level of notes and chords, many technical processes are shared between pop and classical music. The chord pattern known as a cycle of fifths underpins much Baroque music. Musicians of a certain type (perhaps the same ones who like wearing jumpers with holes in them) can extract hours of harmless amusement from trying to spot them in pop and jazz pieces too ('Fly Me to the Moon', 'Les Feuilles Mortes', 'Yellow Brick Road', 'Take Five', 'It's Only Love'). Technical differences are instructive too.

Historical progress in classical music has been charted in terms of the evolving use of dissonance. Pop music, as a very broad generalisation, doesn't use dissonance. Chords are presented straight, and their expressive effect is in their relation to each other. There is no counterpoint, and pop has no equivalent of the symphonic principle, used to roll out and explore abstract musical ideas over an extended span. Could it have? This is a question for later.

Technical processes are the means by which the emotional point is expressed. Being aware of those processes can help explain that point and put it into context, and context gives the process its value. Failure to see music in its context can, as a result, lead to misunderstandings of its value. Or, to put it another way, analysing pop music can turn into a glorious exercise in missing the point. One writer questions the analytical skills of Lady Gaga fans: 'Had they noticed, for example, that Lady Gaga in "Poker Face" stays for most of the tune on one note? Is that real melody?'[139]

Actually, writing a piece that stays on one note is one of the hardest technical challenges a composer or songwriter can set themselves. Cole Porter was particularly keen on seeing how long he could spin the device out ('Night and Day', 'Every Time We Say Goodbye'). Purcell, Britten, Chopin and Brahms all wrote whole pieces or long sections circulating harmony and melody around a single continuous pitch, just as Porter does. (The 'One-Note Samba', on the other hand, isn't actually on one note). Of course repeating a thin snatch of melody over and over again so it gets stuck in your brain is just feeble ('There Must Be an Angel') – no wonder it's called a hook. However, attempts to assess quality through technical analysis must be approached with care, and must respect context. This doesn't mean that 'Poker Face' is as successful and satisfying a work of art as Brahms's *Requiem*, of course it doesn't; or even that it's a particularly good song. But it's not a bad song just because it hangs around one pitch.

These are some of the ways of comparing pop and classical music technically and analytically.[140] They lead into qualitative comparisons. Is one better than the other? The aim of all music is to do what it does well. Different kinds of music set themselves different objectives. Some kinds of music reach further and aim higher. Yet all music succeeds if it has something to say and says it clearly, whether that something is the twilight of the gods or a dreamy lullaby.

Compare Mozart's take on love with Irving Berlin's. The opening duet from *The Marriage of Figaro* mirrors the relationship of the two protagonists, the soon-to-be newly-weds Figaro and Susanna, perfectly. This is not just a function of words, but of the power of form and style to communicate idea. These are real people. Their relationship shifts and changes with the music, as real relationships do. Now look at Irving Berlin's 'You're Just In Love'. It's great – cheeky, cheerful, funny, and true. Yet the range and ambition of its take on human love is a million miles from Mozart's, and deliberately so. This isn't a function of style: it isn't less successful because it's in a jazz idiom; it is because the jazz idiom is not big enough to bear very much reality, and Berlin didn't try to pretend it was.

But it is better jazz. Less serious music can do what it does better than more serious music, even if the what-it-does is less ambitious.

Benjamin Britten and the rock star Pink have both written songs with 'The Truth About Love' in the title. Which tells us more of the truth about love? Britten's is brilliant, facile, arch, coy and suggestive, as you'd expect from a relatively youthful collaboration with poet W. H. Auden. Pink's song, by contrast, is about physical passion and angst. Rock music is certainly better at that (at least in the twentieth century: in the nineteenth it was Wagner).

Another qualitative comparison where different kinds of music can be in direct contrast is in the area where both have to draw on the same resource: words. I think pop music has a better claim to advancing the art of making good words for music in the twentieth century than classical. Ian Dury, Billy Joel, Noël Coward, Jake Thackray and their peers are the poets of modern life, wordsmiths of great subtlety and skill, with more directness and empathy than Auden and Betjeman, and more sheer good humour than you'll find in a month of avant-garde contemporary music programmes in the wasteful watches of the night on Radio 3.

Classical music is more likely to use an existing text. Pop music rarely reaches for the *Oxford Book of English Verse*. An exception is the theatre – operas tend to have newly written libretti, largely for the good practical reason that a libretto needs certain very specific features to do with length, variety and vocal style, which by definition are not those you will readily find in a spoken play. Ronald Duncan describes this aspect well in his book *Working with Britten* about their collaboration on *The Rape of Lucretia*.[141]

Duncan's libretto has been heavily criticised for its verbosity, and whereas this is not the place to pursue that particular critical debate, it does provide a good example of how different kinds of music do things differently. The clunkiness of Duncan's text may very well have been ameliorated by the kind of workshopping and lengthy pre-season off-off-Broadway run routinely given to a major musical. Once again, differences between types of music are not just in the notes but in working practices: the how as well as the what.

The operas of Benjamin Britten show how the success of a work of music-theatre is bound up with the quality of the text. Not all his wordsmiths were as good as they might have been. Nor were Andrew Lloyd Webber's, although his theatre pieces show that success is dependent on more than just the words, but also on a successful alignment between style and substance. *Joseph and the Amazing Technicolour Dreamcoat* is a terrific piece. The wit, tunefulness and sheer good humour match its unpretentious aspirations perfectly.

It works. *Jesus Christ, Superstar* doesn't. The theatrical conceit demands more than the style can give.

An unpretentious style can do unpretentious things perfectly. Noël Coward knew that. 'Extraordinary how potent cheap music is', says Amanda in *Private Lives*, airily. As so often with Coward, it's a wiser and deeper insight than it pretends to be. Read those three simple adjectives backwards – Amanda knows perfectly well that the music wafting over the hotel balcony is cheap, yet she instinctively realises that its very cheapness gives it a potency, a power to carry sentiment and emotion, which more serious music could not do in the same circumstances: and she finds this extraordinary, strange, inexplicable and moving, hinting at something out of reach, something understood. Better music can do more. But it can't do this. Small music can do small things well.

Folk song is the perfection of small music. There's no sadder love-song than 'Bushes and Briars'. Songs like this don't even need accompaniment – words and tune are world enough. Other masters of small music might include Scott Joplin, Arthur Sullivan, Johann Strauss II and John Philip Sousa. The literary equivalent might be a writer like P. G. Wodehouse, who summed up the deliberately limited ambition of the category in an appropriately musical metaphor: 'I believe there are two ways of writing novels. One is making a sort of musical comedy without music and ignoring real life altogether; the other is going deep down into life and not caring a damn.'[142] (Incidentally, Wodehouse was a skilled and prolific lyricist, often collaborating with Jerome Kern, among others). Light music wears its heart on its sleeve. This can be read at an analytical level. Eric Coates's *The Dam Busters March* is a copy of the Elgarian march form. But where Elgar's *Pomp and Circumstance March* no. 5 begins ambiguously in terms of key, almost atonally, and then parcels out its big tune in a controlled, contained way, Coates's gestures are bigger, a bit more obvious. This is partly because the Coates is, to an extent, a deliberate pastiche of the Elgar. But it's more than that. One gives the impression that there is more going on beneath the brass buttons and bristling moustache. It is the bit behind the mask that keeps Elgar interesting.

Pop music can do small too. It is an essentially simpler form than classical music. It comes in two basic types: dance music and the song. Dance music needs a strong regular rhythm. Criticising pop music for rhythmic simplicity is wrong. It wouldn't be much use in a club if it kept chucking in witty little offbeats, Haydn-style. The song is pop at its purest. I use the word here to mean the simplest, oldest and most direct means of musical expression of all – a tune, worked into a shape, fashioned around words, supported by chords. There's something uniquely involving about experiencing words and voice while standing in a puddle of beer at some sweaty late-night town-hall gig. There's a whole playlist of great songs which address exactly this moment of transcendence – 'Piano Man'; 'Killing Me Softly'; 'Mr Tambourine Man' – and that's no coincidence.

While I was writing this book the deaths of two musicians were announced a few days apart. Both made the main evening news bulletins – unusual enough for arty types. By coincidence, their names are close alphabetically, so that when the recording angel finally comes to write up what really happened in our bit of the history of music, these two will sit alongside each other, between Bossanova and Boy George: Pierre Boulez and David Bowie.[143] They make an instructive pair. There are similarities: both were restless experimenters, immune from fads, with a strong dash of the showman. The differences are revealing too, showing up fault lines not just in musical style but in philosophical approach. Boulez approached his own times in the abstract, concerning himself with 'musical technique, which is increasingly concerned with the investigation of a relative world'.[144] Bowie looked his surroundings square in the eye. His authorial voice was the outsider looking in, a spaceman gazing questioningly down from above, a caveman peering up at us from prehistoric depths, or Ziggy Stardust, a sort of cosmic all-of-the-above, a creature outside time and outside gender, Ariel and Prospero rolled into one. The two careers show up different ways of fitting art into life: Boulez's music is important, influential, brilliant and (yes) beautiful; but he was famously unable (or unwilling) to finish anything, and didn't seem to think this was a problem. Bowie made everything part of the artwork, including how, when and where he released an album, and even his own death.

They complement each other. So do the fields in which they worked. There is room for both, and more. Classical music has been around longer. It's more grown up, more developed and more mature. It aims higher and can reach further, infinitely further. But pop music is better pop. It can say things about us which classical music can't (or won't or hasn't).

They are different. And, like different kinds of people, they can and should be valued for what they are, not feared and rejected because of what they're not.

CONCLUSION

Where next? Predictions have always been perilous, not to say foolhardy. One of the few things you can say for certain about innovative creative talent is that you can't say anything about it for certain. But it will come, and it will be a surprise.

If we reached the end of history with *4′33″*, then perhaps the future will need to look back over its shoulder and make some further attempt to incorporate the past. There have certainly been waves of forward-then-back in musical history, but taken overall we have been pretty conservative – same combinations of instruments, same scales, same repetitive rhythmic patterns.

For different styles to meet convincingly you have to reinvent the content. The music of James MacMillan, which deploys musical ideas from the Catholic liturgy and Scottish folk music (among much else) through a thorough technique and a powerful and highly personal sense of poetry, succeeds better in this respect than the music of John Taverner, where the echoes of Orthodox music can, by comparison, sound as though they have been applied to his work like aural decals, rather than reimagined with enough rigour to stand up to their new surroundings.

Styles meeting is a matter of technique as much as substance. Pop-type musical ideas have not generally been subjected to symphonic, contrapuntal, through-composed[145] or other techniques of long-range compositional development familiar to the student of classical music. Why shouldn't they be? The musical ideas might have to adapt, but that's how music evolves. The composer who has got closest to this idea so far is Leonard Bernstein (*Prelude, Fugue and Riffs* is a good example). He addressed the matter in a perceptive preconcert talk in 1958, comparing Milhaud's *La Création du Monde* with Gershwin's *Rhapsody in Blue*: 'in their different ways, they are both doing the same thing: fusing jazz with serious music. Only they came from different sides of the tracks: Gershwin from Tin Pan Alley, and Milhaud from the more sophisticated alleys behind the Eiffel Tower'.[146] The difference shows up not in the tunes or jazzy harmonies, but in the structure – the Milhaud has a coherence based on classical principles, while the Gershwin ends up as a kind of series of musical slabs which you could effectively play in more or less any order you like.

Styles meet where the music stops: Mark-Antony Turnage's viscerally theatrical opera *Greek* and 'We Will Rock You' by Queen both use the same extra-musical gesture, massed stamping feet in a regular pounding rhythm, to illustrate the same thing – the image of a disaffected young man on the edge of urban violence. They sound remarkably similar.

Styles meet when people try their hand at something else: Damon Albarn, Jonny Greenwood, Roger Waters and Paul McCartney are all first-study rockers who have had a stab at oratorio, opera or concerted work.[147] The results don't always pass the Milhaud test – some have enlisted the help of a classically trained assistant or two. But they see no contradiction in liking, and doing, both. Nor should they. Music students today quite happily study Byrd by day and play grunge death metal by night. By contrast, it's a bit hard to imagine Britten or Vaughan Williams in the 1930s spending their evenings playing the washboard in a skiffle band. Perhaps they should have done.

You can also look at this technically. You can read the history of music in an analytical technical way: Charles Rosen said 'The primary means of musical expression is dissonance. This is true at least for Western music since the Renaissance'.[148] And until Schoenberg. Then what? Composers have to a certain extent rowed back from Schoenberg's self-proclaimed 'emancipation of the dissonance',[149] but in doing so they (partly deliberately) limited their options. The music of Britten relies heavily on ostinato. György Ligeti invented something he called micropolyphony, imitating the structural reach of the polyphonic music of the past within a modernist sound-world (a way of moving on from what he revealingly called his 'prehistoric' period).[150] Others reached for the techniques and rhythms of folk music. All involve self-imposed limits as a deliberate way of avoiding existential anarchy and regaining some of the controlling certainty of the past.

Could the forms and structures of classical music be cajoled into an alliance with the sounds of jazz and pop? Could an essentially light, mono-thematic art form like the pop song take on a greater seriousness simply by being imagined on a larger scale? There are analogies in other fields: movies, novels and the theatre were all popular art forms which serious writers explored for their deeper potential. Music can do that. Rodgers and Hammerstein used their own, essentially light, inheritance to create works of serious intent, just as Brecht and Weill did.

Instrumental ensembles could meet across divides. Where is the neo-Baroque concerto grosso for viols, guitars, harpsichord and fretless electric bass? Some contemporary classical composers have hinted at the possibilities of writing for early instruments, but mixing and matching instrumental sounds across genres remains largely the provenance of indie-folk bands like Capercaillie and Stornoway (and they don't tend to play the viol).

What about performance techniques? Players in a gamelan orchestra or percussion ensemble don't read from music, so they look at the conductor. Singers in a choir do read from music, so they look at the music. Why? Why can't the advantages of one be transplanted into the other?

Serious music could do with being less serious. It needs more jokes. Ligeti was good at that, and Berio's wonderful, allusive, all-encompassing *Sinfonia* is funny in a highbrow sort of way, but, generally speaking, modern classical music takes itself terribly seriously. Which recent conservatoire-trained composer can begin to match Mozart, Rossini or Gilbert and Sullivan for lightness and grace? And where is the gift to be simple? Why isn't the composition student at a conservatoire required to compose a song, in a key, without accidentals, on one side of A4, written on two staves, well-structured, with something to say? Britten could have done it. So could Bartók, Vaughan Williams, Maxwell Davies and James MacMillan.[151]

Technology has always influenced music, and always

will. There would be no rock'n'roll without amplification. Technology doesn't just mean electronics – Beethoven's piano, Wagner's tuba, Mozart's clarinet and Ottaviano Petrucci and John Day's printing presses have all had a profound effect on the history of music. But the ability to synthesise and control sound has added something to our idea of what music is. We started with the idea that music is a way of organising a naturally occurring phenomenon (the vibrations of a string or column of air, etc.) In a sense, the ability to manipulate electronic sound removes the restrictions inherent in relying on something which already exists. The body of an electric guitar is designed deliberately not to amplify the string, so that the qualities of the sound are all added electronically, not acoustically. A synthesiser goes further – this is the first musical instrument which doesn't actually produce noise: it produces electronic signals which are then turned into noise. This completely relieves us of the limitations of the natural properties of sound. The basics become not things like an overtone series which occur almost by accident, outside our control, but the properties of sound itself: attack, decay, volume, vibration, pitch in an absolute sense unrelated to a fundamental tone or key. Some of the most interesting and creative early experiments with this kind of manipulation were made with the most basic technology: Karlheinz Stockhausen and Luigi Nono at IRCAM in Paris, Phil Spector and George Martin in the pop studio, using reel-to-reel, scissors and sticky tape. Among the faces on the famous *Sergeant Pepper* album cover are just three musicians, and one of them is Stockhausen.[152] Turns out that all you need is tape.

Recent technological advances include ambient dance music, drum machines and voice benders. The sampler makes electronic sound as much like natural sound as possible. The user can take the actual sound of, for example, an oboe, and make it do whatever he wants it to, including things a human oboist can't (or won't) do. The composer quite literally has the entire palate of a symphony orchestra on the desk (though the one musical sound which has so far proved resistant to this sort of battery-farming is the human voice, which is an interesting comment on the relative complexity and richness of sung and played sound). In a sense progress has gone into reverse – we are using electronics to make ever better copies of acoustic noise, rather than to design new noise (and even back in the 1960s the pioneers of these technologies argued among themselves with theological intensity about whether that was selling out the whole point of electronic music). We still want to listen to the same basic sounds – once again, music is pretty conventional.

Technology can let people make music together even when they're not together. The Last Night of the Proms happens simultaneously inside the Albert Hall and outside, in parks across the UK. Some items in the programme get a continuous performance, moving seamlessly from one end of the country to the other, linked by simultaneous live relay. The American composer Eric Whitacre has set up an online 'virtual choir'. Perhaps one day we really will be able to get the world singing in harmony.

Technology and scholarship also give us access to virtually infinite musical and cultural resources. We can hear, and use, building-blocks that were not available to our pre-decessors, including the scales, modes, and instruments of earlier music and foreign cultures. China had music before we did. India has its ragas, whose complex rhythms fasci-nated Messiaen. Our tradition is the result (or at least the current iteration) of a number of divisions and splits, for example the great East/West schism of Christianity. In a small way, whatever his musical limitations, a composer like John Taverner has reached around that split to bring back in the sounds of Eastern Christianity. What other veils could be torn down?

We have struggled to find a musical voice that speaks for now. When the Berlin wall came down we reached for music written 150 years earlier, the music of Beethoven. Previous generations would not have done this. If we had wanted to mark the event with something new, what kind of music would have been equal to the task? Arvo Pärt? U2? Has contemporary classical music written itself out of the script? Those of us who care about and value its capacity for beauty and renewal have to worry about that. Classi-cal music has to find a way to stop talking to itself. It has to find new things, good things, to be about. John Adams has taken the bold step of putting contemporary political figures on stage in works like *Nixon in China* and *The Death of Klinghoffer*. His work makes the operas of Philip Glass sound even more like pompous twaddle than they already do. There's little doubt which represents the more serious attempt to bring the intellectual inheritance of Western art music to bear on the contemporary world.

This discussion began with the question of what music

is. Perhaps that has turned out to be what Charles Ives called *The Unanswered Question.* The author Philip Ball begins his insightful book on music like this: 'Hadn't I better explain what I am talking about, when I am talking about music? That would seem a sensible preliminary, but I am going to decline it.'[153] Does that make me more or less sensible than Ball? I have at least tried to answer the question. My answer is certainly wrong, in the sense that no answer is immune from exceptions and partialities, and it is centred too much in the music I know, which means Western music. Another writer comments perceptively that a book of this kind can be read as a sort of 'map that all music could in principle be put on to.'[154] If it is, it's like one of those medieval maps that has the West at the centre of the world, and reveals more about the cartographer's ignorance and prejudice than it does about the territory being surveyed. Let's take the analogy a little further: a modern map is much more accurate. If you lived in, say, Mexico, and decided to visit Dorset, and you're planning a walk from, say, Sturminster Newton to Piddletrenthide, the Ordnance Survey 1:10,000 series will tell you everything you need to know, including the difference between a church with a spire and a church with a steeple and the location of the nearest pub. But will it tell you what it is actually like to walk across those clouded hills, to see that massy tower looming out of the mist, step through the flinty porch to donate sixpence and then nip next door for a pint of Old Peculier by the fire? Not even slightly. Reading about a piece of music 'does not lead us to savour whatever distinctive voice the composer may have had … one might as well study a train timetable and hope to gain therefrom a clear picture of the landscapes that will accompany one's journeys', as Donald Mitchell sagely observed.[155] (Though there is, in fact, an inherent musicality in an English railway timetable – listen to 'The Slow Train' by Flanders and Swann).

So I hope you will accept Philip Ball's maxim that 'In a subject of this nature, ideas and views that differ from one's own should not be targets for demolition, but whetstones for sharpening one's own thoughts.'[156] To take that one stage further – if you have disagreed with my judgments, then so much the better. I hope at least you may have discovered some music along the way which you found interesting and worth getting to know.

I have tried not to use words in ways which seem designed to set the writer about music apart from the reader, like using music as a plural, or with an indefinite article, or in inverted commas or italics. After all, the most accurate aphorisms about music neatly make the point that words just won't hack it – 'It's not that music is too imprecise for words, but too precise' (Mendelssohn);[157] 'if you have to ask, you'll never know' (Louis Armstrong);[158] 'music can name the unnameable and communicate the unknowable' (Leonard Bernstein);[159] 'writing about music is like dancing about architecture' (Elvis Costello);[160] 'music would take over at the point at which words become powerless' (Debussy);[161] 'say it with music' (Irving Berlin).[162]

We are back where we started. We are back inside your brain, making patterns: 'only connect', pleaded E. M. Forster.[163] We are back with organised sound: in the 1950s the architect-musicians Le Corbusier, Edgard Varèse and

Iannis Xenakis combined built and heard form in 'an Electronic Poem and a vessel containing the poem; light, colour, image, rhythm and sound joined together in an organic synthesis', in the same way that the medieval mind applied the Golden Section and other mathematical relationships to the structural organisation of both architecture and music.

We are back with sound as nature, as described by the first, and best, of the philosopher-musicians. In 1968 Karlheinz Stockhausen wrote a piece in which six singers conjure up the overtones of a fundamental B flat for about 75 minutes. He called the piece *Stimmung*, which, according to the composer, 'means "tuning", but it really should be translated with many other words because *Stimmung* incorporates the meanings of the tuning of a piano, the tuning of the voice, the tuning of a group of people, the tuning of the soul. This is all in the German word. Also, when you say: We're in a good *Stimmung*, you mean a good psychological tuning, being well tuned together.'[164] This is the language of Pythagoras. Were these the sounds he heard on his mountain-top two-and-a-half millennia ago, when doing his 'soul-adjustments'? It may be as close as we're going to get.

We're back with the music of the spheres. Theoretical physicist Dr Michio Kaku says 'In string theory, all particles are vibrations on a tiny rubber band; physics is the harmonies on the string; chemistry is the melodies we play on vibrating strings; the universe is a symphony of strings, and the "Mind of God" is cosmic music resonating in eleven-dimensional hyperspace.'[166] In that awesome and ineffable concept the image of Plato measuring out the heavens with music comes full circle. That's no coincidence. Nor is the fact that Kaku reaches for mystical language to describe what he sees, like a mixture of Thomas Cranmer and Obi-Wan Kenobi. Music helps us to see not 'through a glass, darkly', but to look at both the universe and ourselves 'face to face'.[167] All attempts to understand the human condition are about making patterns.

How does music let us unweave its secrets? Learn about it, then forget what you've learned. Be critically engaged, but be open to everything. Take the same approach to music as you do to people – be liberal. Be inquisitive, be informed, then listen. Just listen.

FURTHER RESOURCES AND INVESTIGATIONS

I have tried to mention below a small number of works which seem to me to address an aspect of the art, philosophy, context and development of music in an interesting way, rather than books about particular composers or periods, or works of pure history. Any attempt to provide a listening list would either have to include everything or be meaninglessly selective, so I've ducked that particular challenge. I hope readers will feel inspired to follow the signposts in the text and set off to discover music they don't know, online, in the record shop, or better still by going to hear it live, and best of all by making music yourself.

Key texts about where music might possibly have come from are Steven Pinker, *The Language Instinct* (New York: W. Morrow and Co, 1994), and Steven Brown, Nils Lennart Wallin, Björn Merker, *The Origins of Music* (MIT Press, 2001). A fascinating narrative of how music might have moved through prehistory (and a great title) is Gary Tomlinson, *A Million Years of Music: the emergence of human modernity* (MIT Press, 2015).

Moving into history, two writers who combine scholarship with the insights of the top-drawer performer are John Butt, whose *Playing with History: the historical approach to musical performance* (*Musical Performance and Reception*)

(Cambridge University Press, 2002) is an academic account of the philosophy behind 'historically informed performance', and Charles Rosen, the best, most accessible and most enduring chronicler of musical style, how it works and what it is. See in particular *The Classical Style: Haydn, Mozart, Beethoven* (London: Faber, 1976); and *Sonata Forms* (New York: Norton, 1988).

A stimulating discussion of the role of the written score and the work in performance, along with much else of interest and value, is Richard Taruskin, *Text and Act: essays on music and performance*, (New York: Oxford University Press, 1995). For a scholar deciding what's good and bad, and why (and for some classic put-downs of composers he doesn't like), see Joseph Kerman, *Opera as Drama* (Westport, Conn: Greenwood Press, 1981).

Music in the twentieth century has generated plenty of words, words, words, as Hamlet put it. I've picked two accounts of two different ways through the wood, by two men who were there: Charles Rosen, *Schoenberg* (London: Marion Boyars, 1976; distributed by Calder and Boyars), on the work, thoughts, life and legacy of the man who made music move away from tonality; and Leonard Bernstein's classic apologia for music which didn't – *The Unanswered Question: a series of six lectures,* given in 1973. The lectures were published in book form by Harvard University Press in 1997, but are probably best experienced in the format in which he gave them, to be found at www.youtube.com/watch?v=MB7ZOdp__gQ (lecture 1, with links to lectures 2–6).

A brilliantly perceptive and sympathetic account of

the good, the bad and the ugly in contemporary classical music in the Glock/Darmstadt years is Donald Mitchell, *The Language of Modern Music* (London: Faber and Faber, 1963). Mitchell was Benjamin Britten's publisher, and was thus responsible for issuing in book form the speech Britten gave in 1964 *On Receiving the First Aspen Award* (Faber and Faber, 1982): the thoughts of a master, all the more precious because he rarely spoke publicly about his art (unlike some). An overview of the last hundred-and-a-bit years which has already become a classic, by a classical critic who also loves and values rock music, is Alex Ross, *The Rest is Noise: listening to the twentieth century* (HarperCollins UK, 2009).

Recent publishing activity has produced some stimulating discussions of what music is, and its context in the society and intellectual and artistic currents of our times. The view of an academic can be found in Nicholas Cook, *Music: a very short introduction* (Oxford University Press, USA, 2000); that of a practitioner in David Byrne, *How Music Works* (Canongate Books, 2013).

Writers who have addressed how music fits with the wider human personality and the functioning of the mind include Anthony Storr in *Music and the Mind* (HarperCollins Publishers Ltd, 1997), and James Rhodes in his moving memoir *Instrumental* (Canongate Books, 2015).

Finally, there has been a succession of excellent recent generalist accounts of the ideas behind music, scientific, philosophical and historical, in particular Philip Ball, *The Music Instinct: how music works and why we can't do without it*, (Random House, 2011) whose title neatly takes us back to where this list started.

SOURCES AND REFERENCES

INTRODUCTION

1   *Merchant of Venice*, Act V, sc. 1
2   *Julius Caesar*, Act I, sc. 2
3   1 Samuel 16: 14 and 23
4   Iamblichus, 'Life of Pythagoras' (*c.* 250–300), quoted in, for example, Kenneth Sylvan Guthrie, *The Pythagorean Sourcebook and Library: an anthology of ancient writings which relate to Pythagoras and Pythagorean philosophy* (US: Phanes Press, 1988), p. 72
5   Plato, *Republic*, III 401d–e
6   Job, 38: 4 and 7
7   Genesis, 4: 21
8   Boethius, *De Institutione Musica*, Book 1, Introduction
9   Confucius, quoted for example in the chapter 'China' by Wai-Chung Ho in Liora Bresler, *International Handbook of Research in Arts Education*, 2 volume set (Springer, 2007), p. 52
10 John Dryden, from 'A Song for Saint Cecilia's Day', 1687
11 William Collins, from 'The Passions: an ode for music'
12 Lord Byron, from *Don Juan*, Canto the Fifteenth
13 Sir Walter Scott, quoted in 'Thoughts on Music', in *The Southern Literary Messenger*, vol. vii (Richmond: Thomas White, 1841)
14 See Charles Darwin, *The Descent of Man* (1871), ch. 3, section 13 (Language): 'When we treat of sexual selection we shall see that primeval man, or rather some early progenitor of man, probably first used his voice in producing true musical cadences, that is in singing, as do some of the gibbon-apes at the present day; and we may conclude from a widely spread analogy, that this power would have been especially exerted during the courtship of the sexes – would have expressed various emotions, such as love, jealousy, triumph – and would have served as a challenge to rivals. It is, therefore, probable that the imitation of musical cries by articulate sounds may have given rise to words expressive of various complex emotions.'
15 From Tippett's notes to his oratorio, *The Vision of St Augustine*, 1965
16 New Seekers, 'I'd Like to Teach the World to Sing (In Perfect Harmony)', by Bill Backer, Billy Davis, Roger Cook and Roger Greenaway (1971)

17　T. S. Eliot, from 'Little Gidding', in *Four Quartets* (London: Faber & Faber, 2001)

18　T. S. Eliot, from *The Family Reunion* (London: Faber & Faber Inc, 1939)

1. WHAT IS MUSIC?

19　Samuel Johnson, *A Dictionary of the English Language*, 1755

20　Thomas Hobbes, *Leviathan*(1665), Chapter 9

2. WHAT IS A PIECE OF MUSIC?

21　See, for example, Piano Concerto no. 24 in C minor, K 491, mt 1, bars 261/262

22　Schoenberg's Piano Pieces, op 11, no. 2, bars 11 and 12; String Quartet no. 2, op. 10, mt 1 ('etwas langsamer anfangen …')

23　See, for example, the manuscript of Piano Concerto no. 15 in B flat major, K 450, available in facsimile here: http://petrucci.mus.auth.gr/imglnks/ usimg/0/0f/IMSLP292831-PMLP15373-Mozart_-_Concerto_in_B_per_il_ Piano_Forte_-K450-.pdf

24　Beethoven: 'with the most deeply felt expression'; marking for the third movement of the Piano Sonata no. 30, op. 109

25　See, for example, Paul Kildea, *Benjamin Britten: A Life in the Twentieth Century*, Part 7, chapter 1 (London: Penguin UK, 2013)

26　The words are on his gravestone in Rome, put there on his death in February 1821 by his friends Joseph Severn, Charles Brown and others, apparently at his own request.

27　Keats again, from 'Ode on a Grecian Urn' (1819)

3. THE HISTORIES OF MUSIC

28　For an introduction to the science of archeo-acoustics, see for example the article by Ker Than in *National Geographic*, July 2008

29　Images of the statues are readily available online. For a timeline and discussion of their origins, see *World Archaeology*, Issue 48 (6 July 2011). For a detailed account of the Keros discoveries, see Colin Renfrew, 'The Sanctuary at Keros: Questions of Materiality and Monumentality', *Journal of the British Academy*, 1, 187–212 (December 2013)

30 See David Wulstan, 'The Earliest Musical Notation', *Music and Letters* 52 (1971), 365–82; and Martin Litchfield West, 'The Babylonian Musical Notation and the Hurrian Melodic Texts', *Music and Letters* 75, no. 2 (May 1994), 161–79. Images are available online, as are recordings of speculative reconstructions of what the songs sound like

31 See John G. Landels, *Music in Ancient Greece and Rome* (London: Routledge, 1998). Again, images, modern transcriptions and recordings can be found online

32 For a good introduction, with pictures, see the article 'Flutes offer clues to Stone Age Music' in the *New York Times*, 24 June 2009: http://www. nytimes.com/2009/06/25/science/25flute.html?_r=0

33 See Diarmaid MacCulloch, *A History of Christianity: the first three thousand years* (London: Allen Lane, 2009), pp. 158–9

34 Psalm 81, v. 3

35 See, for example, 'The World's Most Musical Languages' by John McWhorter in *The Atlantic*, 13 November 2015

36 See Andrew Gant, *O Sing Unto the Lord: a history of English church music* (London: Profile, 2015), chs. 2–6

37 Lydia Goehr, *The Imaginary Museum of Musical Works: an essay in the philosophy of music,* revised edition (Oxford University Press, USA, 2007)

38 See for example David Huron, *Sweet Anticipation: music and the psychology of expectation* (Cambridge, Mass: MIT Press, 2006), p. 352

39 Joseph Kerman, *Opera as Drama* (Westport, Conn: Greenwood Press, 1956), p. 264

40 See 'Facing up, finally, to Bach's dark vision' in Richard Taruskin, *Text and Act: essays on music and performance* (New York: Oxford University Press, 1995)

41 For Peter Hall's account of Margaret Thatcher's reaction to Peter Shaffer's play *Amadeus*, see article 'She may not have known it, but even Thatcher was not immune to art's capacity to challenge', by David Lister, *Independent*, 13 April 2013

42 Malcolm Gladwell, *Outliers: The Story of Success* (UK: Penguin, 2008), p. 17

43 This form of words was used by Rhodes on BBC Radio 3's *In Tune* on 25 September 2015. The idea is expanded in his *Guardian* article 'Forget the mad genius composer myth: music is good for the mind' (19 September 2015), both referring to his book *Instrumental* (Canongate, 2015)

4. HOW MUSIC WORKS

44 See Emilio Audissino (2014) *John Williams's Film Music: Jaws, Star Wars, Raiders of the Lost Ark, and the Return of the Classical Hollywood Music Style* (University of Wisconsin Press, 2014), p. 71

45 Like many well-known aphorisms, versions of this saying have been attributed to all sorts of people. The attribution to Stravinsky is in Peter Yates, *Twentieth Century Music; Its Evolution from the End of the Harmonic Era into the Present Era of Sound* (New York: Pantheon Books, A Division of Random House, 1967), p. 41, where Yates claims to have heard the remark from Stravinsky himself. It's the sort of thing Stravinsky might have said (or might have liked to have been believed to have said), but then, like other coiners of bon-mots, witty quotes gather round his reputation both with and without authority

46 See BBC News report, http://www.bbc.co.uk/news/entertainment-arts-36611961

47 Very widely quoted (sometimes with reference to one or more other pieces of Brahms), but, like many quotations originating from a conversation, difficult to pin down to an original first source

48 Percy Alfred Scholes, *The Oxford Companion to Music* (London: Oxford University Press, 1938), under 'Melody', p. 622

49 With thanks to Daniel Pugh-Beavan

50 Donald Mitchell, *The Language of Modern Music* (London: Faber and Faber, 1963), p. 128

51 Scholes, ibid.

52 I am grateful to Rick Blaskey, who effected the transformation of Holst's tune to rugby anthem, for verifying this paragraph and permission to use the story

5. HOW WE USE MUSIC

53 See http://www.john-jacob-niles.com/music.htm

54 I am grateful to the singer and music educationalist Katrina Hicks Beach (John Levy's great-niece) for these insights. For further information about the John Levy archive see: http://www.ed.ac.uk/literatures-languages-cultures/celtic-scottish-studies/archives/archive-projects/john-levy-archive For an interesting essay on Japanese musical westernisation: http://cejsh.icm.edu.pl/cejsh/element/bwmeta1.element.desklight-29567af0-b385-490d-add4-e8a106208299/c/Gaspar_v02.pdf

55 See 'Sgioba Luaidh Inbhirchluaidh' at www.waulk.org

56 Roger Scruton, 'Why it's time to turn the music off', BBC Radio 4, *A Point of View* (13 Nov 2015), at http://www.bbc.co.uk/news/magazine-34801885

57 Thomas Morley, 'A plaine and easie Introduction to Practicall musicke' (London, 1597)

58 James Hamilton-Paterson, 'The Music (I)' in the short story collection *The Music* (London: Jonathan Cape, 1995), p. 2

59 This story is from the early biography of Beethoven by his secretary, Ferdinand Ries

60 See Erin Runions, *The Babylon Complex: Theopolitical fantasies of war, sex and sovereignty* (New York: Fordham University Press, 2014), p. 152. See also Clive Stafford Smith, 'Welcome to "the disco"', *Guardian*, 19 June 2008. For Bournemouth and Alvin and the Chipmunks, see 'Police play novelty cartoon music at Travel Interchange to deter homeless people', article by Toby Wadey in the *Bournemouth Echo*, 3 December 2015

61 See Nick Rossi, *Domenico Cimarosa: his life and his operas* (Westport, Conn: Greenwood Press, 1999)

62 See 'Teenagers', by My Chemical Romance

63 See, for example, Kerry Robin McCarthy, *Byrd* (New York: Oxford University Press, 2013)

64 See, for example, Solomon Volkov, *Shostakovich and Stalin: the extraordinary relationship between the great composer and the brutal dictator* (New York: Knopf, 2004), ch. 6

65 For a discussion of this and other pairings of the work, see Joy H. Calico, *Arnold Schoenberg's 'A Survivor from Warsaw' in Post-war Europe* (Berkeley: University of California Press, 2014), p. 3 et seq.

66 See www.thecalaissessions.com

67 See Humphrey Carpenter, *Benjamin Britten: a biography* (London: Faber and Faber, 1992); p. 198 ('The Ballad of Little Musgrave and Lady Barnard'); and pp. 226–7 (concerts in camps with Yehudi Menuhin)

68 Messaien 'Quatuor pour la fin du temps' composed in Stalag VIII-A, 1943, see Rebecca Rischin, *For the End of Time: The Story of the Messiaen Quartet* (Cornell University Press, 2003), p. 62

69 In *An Account of a Conversation concerning a right regulation of Governments for the common good of Mankind* (1703)

6. HOW WE LEARN ABOUT MUSIC

70 Iona Archibald Opie, *The Lore and Language of Schoolchildren* (New York: New York Review Books, 2001)

71 Locke: 'Some Thoughts Concerning Education' (1693), section 2

72 I am grateful to the pianist concerned for permission to use this story

73 Related by the composer to Robert Buckley. See Daniel M. Grimley, Julian Rushton, *The Cambridge Companion to Elgar* (Cambridge University Press, 2004), ch. 4

74 See 'I turned down McCartney', article in the *Liverpool Echo*, 30 April 2008

75 Geoffrey Willans, Ronald Searle, *Back in the Jug Agane* (UK: Penguin, 2009)

76 Stravinsky: another apt and much-quoted aphorism of uncertain provenance

77 L. P. Hartley, *The Go-Between* (London: Penguin, 1970), ch. 1

78 J. L. Carr, *A Month in the Country* (London: Penguin, 1980)

79 Stravinsky, modernism and neoclassicism: see John Butt, *Playing with History: the historical approach to musical performance (Musical Performance and Reception)* (Cambridge University Press, 2002), ch. 5

80 Bill Bryson, *Notes from a Small Island* (UK: Transworld Publ. Limited, 2015), p. 166

81 See in particular Nicholas Temperley, 'Performing practice: the clef problem' in *The Music of the English Parish Church* (London: Cambridge University Press, 1979), pp. 184–90

82 John Keats, 'Lamia', Part II (1820), line 230 et seq.

83 Teaching-manuals: Thomas Morley, 'A plaine and easie Introduction to Practicall musicke'; Fux, Johann Joseph, *Gradus ad Parnassum* (1725); Mozart, W. A., Theoretical and Compositional Studies for Thomas Attwood, K. 506a, (Kassel: Barenreiter-Verlag, 1965), Mozart complete edition, Series X, 30/1, BA 4543-01; Schoenberg, Arnold, *Fundamentals of Musical Composition* (London: Faber and Faber, 1967)

84 See, for example *D. C. Gilman, H. T. Thurston, F. M. Colby (eds.) 'Quadrivium', New International Encyclopedia* (1st edn.) (New York: Dodd, Mead, 1905)

85 *Elizabeth I: in the 1559 Injunctions. See* Andrew Gant, *O Sing Unto the Lord: a history of English church music* (London: Profile, 2015), p. 105

86 Thomas Hobbes, *Leviathan*, Chapter 9

87 Samuel Johnson, *A Dictionary of the English Language* (1755)

88 Charles Dickens, *Bleak House* (1852–3), ch. 49

89 Michael Freedland (1986) *A Salute to Irving Berlin* (London: W. H. Allen, 1986), p. 128

90 See Hunter Davies, *Hunting People: Thirty Years of Interviews With the Famous* (Edinburgh: Mainstream Publishing, 1995). McCartney says: 'I can't really play the piano, or read or write music. I've tried three times in my life to learn, but never kept it up for more than three weeks. The last bloke I went to was great. I'm sure he could teach me a lot. I might go back to him. It's just the notation – the way you write down notes. It doesn't look like music to me.'

91 Sir James H. Jeans (fp 1937) *Science and Music* (Courier Corporation ed, 2012), p. 152

92 Thomas Edison, Spoken statement (*c.* 1903); published in *Harper's Monthly* (September 1932).

93 The Beatles and technical devices: see also note 17 in chapter 8 below

94 'Double' songs (sometimes known as 'counter-melody songs'): one singer sings a verse to one tune, then a second singer sings a second verse to a different tune, then the two are combined and sung simultaneously. The trick is to make all three sections work equally well. A good example is 'You're Just in Love'

95 The Rolling Stones (1974) 'I Know It's Only Rock'n'Roll…' Jagger/Richards

96 This Stravinsky quote is verifiable, or at least has a source: *Observer*, 8 October 1961

7. HOW WE TALK ABOUT MUSIC

97 Quoted in Peter Eckermann's *Conversations with Goethe*. The phrase had been used earlier, by Friedrich von Schelling, in *Philosophie der Kunst*: '[Architecture] is music in space, as it were a frozen music.'

98 See John Bridcut, *Essential Britten* (London: Faber and Faber, 2012), ch. 5

99 Interview (1959) 'Back to Britain with Britten', reprinted in Benjamin Britten, *Britten on Music* (Oxford: Oxford University Press, 2003), p. 171

100 Diary entry, 9 October 1886

101 See, for example, Alan Blyth, *Remembering Britten* (London: Hutchinson, 1981), p. 88

102 Letter (22 April 1914), declining the invitation to compose a work in honour of Strauss's fiftieth birthday. See Arnold Schoenberg, *Arnold Schoenberg letters* (Berkeley: University of California Press, 1987), p. 51

103 Schoenberg quotes this remark in the same letter, as one of his reasons for refusal. Strauss made the remark in a letter to Frau [Alma] Mahler

104 The comment was passed to Stravinsky by Auden, the librettist. Stravinsky was apparently 'not amused'. See Humphrey Carpenter, *Benjamin Britten: a biography* (London: Faber and Faber, 1992), p. 297

105 Another widely quoted aphorism of uncertain provenance. See for example the article 'Musical Marathon' in *The Independent*, 1 March 2006, which gives a date of 1867

106 The radio executive was Darren Henley of Classic fm. I am grateful for his permission to include this passage

107 *The Blues Brothers* (1980), director John Landis

108 See Thomas Vautor *Sweet Suffolk Owl*; Delius *On Hearing the First Cuckoo in Spring*; Rautavaara *Cantus Arcticus*; Stornoway 'Boom Went the Bittern'

109 Vivaldi, *Le Quatro Staggioni*; Beethoven, *Pastoral* Symphony; Verdi, *Otello* (and *Rigoletto*); Britten, *Peter Grimes*

110 *Archbishop Parker's Psalter* (1567), see Gant, *O Sing Unto the Lord*, p. 112

111 Erik Routley, *The Musical Wesleys* (London: Herbert Jenkins,1968), pp. 26–7

112 See in particular 'Un amour de Swann', Part II of *Du côté de chez Swann*, though the 'petit phrase' recurs throughout *A la recherche du temps perdu*, particularly in relation to Swann's relationship with Odette.

113 'Many writers have ascribed masculine and feminine features to the two themes of sonata form…'; for example, the composer Vincent d'Indy, quoted in Nicholas Cook, *Music: A Very Short Introduction (Very Short Introductions)* (USA: Oxford University Press, 2000), pp. 109–10

114 Charles Rosen, *The Classical Style: Haydn, Mozart, Beethoven* (London: Faber, 1976), p. 30

115 This debate was stirred up in certain circles by the American musicologist Susan McClary in her book *Feminine Endings: music, gender, and sexuality: with a new introduction* (Minneapolis: University of Minnesota Press, 1991). You can, if you wish, trace the arguments for and against her thesis in Cook, *Music*, pp. 117–22, and Philip Ball, *The Music Instinct: how music works and why we can't do without it* (Random House, 2011), pp. 388–95

116 Deryck Cooke, *The Language of Music* (Oxford: Oxford University Press, 1990)

117 Adorno (fp 1947): see Theodor W. Adorno, tr. Anne G. Mitchell, Wesley V. Blomster, *Philosophy of Modern Music* (Bloomsbury Publishing, 2007), p. 25

118 Francis Fukuyama, *The End of History and the Last Man* (New York: Free Press, 1992)

119 The phrase is McClary's (op. cit.)

120 Aaron Copland, ed. Richard Kostelanetz, *Aaron Copland: a reader: selected writings 1923–1972* (New York: Routledge, 2004), p. 4

121 See, for example, David Lidov, *Is Language a Music?: Writings on Musical Form and Signification (Musical Meaning and Interpretation)* (Indiana University Press, 2004)

122 See McWhorter, op. cit.

123 S. Brown, 'The "Musilanguage" Model of Music Evolution' in N. L. Wallin, B. Merker and S. Brown, *The Origins of Music* (The MIT Press, 1999), pp. 271–301

124 Included on the album *The Doughnut in Granny's Greenhouse* (1968)

8. HOW MUSIC TALKS ABOUT US

125 On being turned down for the Pulitzer Prize, 1965. See Nat Hentoff, *At the Jazz Band Ball: sixty years on the jazz scene* (Berkeley: University of California Press, 2010), p. 23

126 See Mark Tucker, Duke Ellington, *The Duke Ellington Reader* (Oxford University Press, 1993), p. 326

127 For older and newer music gestures in the same piece, see for example 'O God, thou art my God' by Purcell and the Monteverdi *Mass* for four voices

128 Critics and theorists played their part in the theological debates at Darmstadt, too: a sort of musical Council of Trent. See (among much else): Hans Werner.Henze, *Music and Politics: Collected Writings, 1953–1981*. Translated by Peter Labanyi (Ithaca: Cornell University Press, 1982); Christopher Fox, 'Luigi Nono and the Darmstadt School', *Contemporary Music Review* 18/2 (1999), 111–30; Martin Iddon, *New Music at Darmstadt: Nono, Stockhausen, Cage, and Boulez (Music since 1900)* (Cambridge and New York: Cambridge University Press, 2013)

129 Reported remark, 1920. See for example the chapter on Bartok's string quartets in Lucy Miller Murray, 'Chamber Music' (New York: Roman and Littlefield, 2015), p. 28

130 In the article 'Contre la paresse' ['Against laziness'] in *La Page Musicale*, 17 March 1939. See Messiaen, Olivier, *Olivier Messiaen: journalism 1935–1939* (Burlington, VT: Ashgate, 2012), p. 68

131 In the 'They Said It' column, *Daily Telegraph*, 30 March 1996

132 Freedland, op. cit.

133 In a broadcast interview widely quoted in his obituaries. See for example the *Independent*, 14 March 2016

134 Larkin, in his *Paris Review* interview. See Philip Gourevitch, *The Paris Review Interviews* (Canongate Books, 2007), p. 231

135 In Charles Rosen, *Schoenberg* (London: Marion Boyars, 1976), p. 58: ' … each individual line in Schoenberg's music … defines a harmonic sense that, *even when transposed*, can fit into the general harmony of the work as a whole.'

136 Quoted by Rosen in Charles Rosen, *Critical Entertainments: music old and new* (Harvard University Press, 2000), p. 312

137 The piano piece in question is the Rondo movement of Sonatina in G major, op. 36, no. 5

138 For a first-hand account of this aspect, see Davies, op. cit.

139 Scruton, op. cit.

140 The Beatles were highly amused at attempts to analyse their music academically: they used to point out 'Aeolian cadences' in their own songs to each other because a critic had spotted one, even though they had no idea what it was. Of course, it is entirely legitimate to notice and point out the different modes in Beatles songs ('Love Me Do' is in the Dorian, for example). Wilfrid Mellers and others did pioneering work in getting writers about music to look seriously at how a good pop song works. Today, according to a recent BBC report, many young people think of the Beatles as classical performers. *Sic transit …* See Hunter Davies, *The Beatles Lyrics: The unseen story behind their music* (London: Weidenfeld & Nicolson, 2014), p. 57

141 Ronald Duncan, *Working with Britten: a personal memoir* (Bideford: The Rebel Press, 1981)

142 Quoted for example in Professor Ann Rea (ed.), *Middlebrow Wodehouse* (Ashgate, 2016), ch. 4

143 Pierre Boulez died 5 January 2016. David Bowie died 10 January 2016.

144 Pierre Boulez, *Orientations: collected writings* (Cambridge, MA: Harvard University Press, 1986), p. 143

CONCLUSION

145 'Through-composed' music has a continuously evolving structure through an entire movement or piece, by contrast with, for example, a strophic song which builds up its structure by repeating passages of music a number of times

146 Quoted for example in Ryan Raul Bañagale, *Arranging Gershwin: Rhapsody in Blue and the creation of an American icon* (New York: Oxford University Press, 2014), p. 94

147 The classical works by rock musicians include: *Dr Dee*, opera with music by Albarn (2011); Greenwood, *48 responses to Polymorphia*, a collaboration with Krzysztof Penderecki; Waters, *Ça Ira*, opera (2005); McCartney, *Standing Stones*, an oratorio (1997)

148 Charles Rosen, *Schoenberg* (London: Marion Boyars, 1976), p. 32

149 Arnold Schoenberg, *Style and Idea*, p. 104

150 See Richard Steinitz, *György Ligeti: music of the imagination* (Boston: Northeastern University Press, 2003), ch. 2: typically, the remark is used in a spirit of humorous self-mockery

151 As evidence for my claims for these composers' ability to be simple, I give you 'A New Year Carol'; *Mikrokosmos*; 'Linden Lea'; 'Farewell to Stromness'; and MacMillan's congregational Mass settings

152 For the influence of Stockhausen on the Beatles in the *Sergeant Pepper* period, see Davies, op cit., p. 3

153 Philip Ball, *The Music Instinct* (Random House, 2011), p. 9

154 Cook, op. cit., Foreword

155 Mitchell, op. cit., pp. 164–5

156 Ball, op. cit., Preface

157 Letter to Marc-André Souchay, 15 October 1842, cited from *Briefe aus den Jahren 1830 bis 1847* (Leipzig: Hermann Mendelssohn, 1878), p. 221. The German reads: '*Das, was mir eine Musik ausspricht, die ich liebe, sind mir nicht zu* unbestimmte *Gedanken, um sie in Worte zu fassen, sondern zu* bestimmte.'

158 Reply when Armstrong was asked to define the rhythmic concept of 'swing', quoted in John F. Szwed, *Jazz 101: a complete guide to learning and loving jazz,* (Hachette Books, 2000). Another of those universal tag-quotes that's been said by, or at least attributed to, lots of people, about lots of things

159 In his series of six lectures under the title 'The Unanswered Question', given at Harvard, 1973

160 In an interview for *New Musical Express*, 25 March 1978. Costello appears to have been the first to use this particular version of the saying in print, though it had been around in various forms for most of the twentieth century

161 See for example Paul Holmes, *Debussy* (London: Book Sales Ltd, 1989), p. 36

162 'Say it with Music', as above

163 Epigraph to *Howard's End*: expanded in the novel as 'only connect the prose and the passion, and both will be exalted, and human love will be seen at its height'

164 Jonathan Cott, *Stockhausen: Conversations with the Composer* (New York: Simon and Schuster, 1973), p. 162

165 Kaku, in an online lecture connected with his book *The Future of the Mind* (2015)

166 1 Corinthians 13: 12

INDEX

A

Adams, John 37; *The Death of Klinghoffer* 127; *Nixon in China* 127
Adorno, Theodor 94, 96
Albarn, Damon 122
Allen, Woody: *Manhattan* 105
Alvin and the Chipmunks 63
ancient civilisations 25
Armstrong, Louis 129
Auden, W. H. 115
Augustine, St 5
Austen, Jane 37, 104

B

Bach, Carl Philipp Emmanuel 79
Bach, Johann Sebastian 16, 22, 35, 45, 49, 72, 75, 76, 77, 79, 87, 107
    Fantasia in G major *(Pièce d'orgue)* 44
    Two-part Invention no. 1 in C major 49
    Prelude in D major from *The Well-Tempered Clavier Book 1* 94
Ball, Philip 128, 129, 135
Barenboim, Daniel 65
Baring-Gould, Rev. Sabine 71
Barney the Purple Dinosaur 63
Bartók, Béla 37, 106, 107, 124
Beatles, The 18, 69, 80, 81, 105, 111
    'It's Only Love' 80, 113
    'Lady Madonna' 80
    Sgt. Pepper's Lonely Hearts Club Band 125
    'Yesterday' 17

Beethoven, Ludwig van 21, 30, 32, 34, 45, 60, 76, 86, 89, 91, 99, 106, 108, 127
    Fidelio 61
    Violin Concerto 61
    Piano Sonata no. 8 *(Pathétique)* 95
    Piano Sonata no. 12 61
    Piano Concerto no. 5 *(Emperor)* 62
    Symphony no. 1 44
    Symphony no. 3 62
    Symphony no. 9 41, 65
    Wellington's Victory March 62
Bennett, Richard Rodney: *Murder on the Orient Express* 85
Berio, Luciano: *Sinfonia* 124
Berlin, Irving 79, 80, 107, 129
    'You're Just In Love' 115
Berlioz, Hector 34
Bernstein, Leonard 80, 129
    Kaddish Symphony 65
    Prelude, Fugue and Riffs 122
Betjeman, John 115
Biber, Heinrich 72
Birtwistle, Harrison 32, 107
Bliss, Arthur 11
Blondel 34
Blues Brothers, The (film) 86
Boethius 3
'Bohemian Rhapsody' 87
Bonzo Dog Doo-Dah Band, The 101
Bootleg Beatles, The (band) 75
Boulanger, Nadia 39
Boulez, Pierre 106, 119

Bowie, David 119
Boy George 119
Brahms, Johannes 30, 77, 84, 86, 106, 114
   Ein Deutsches Requiem 114
   Symphony no. 1 41
Bridge, Frank 39
Britten, Benjamin 22, 31, 37, 39, 65, 83, 84, 89, 106, 114, 123, 124
   Night Mail 85
   The Rape of Lucretia 116
   'Tell Me the Truth About Love' 115
   The Young Person's Guide to the Orchestra 46
Brown, James 56
Brown, Steven 101
Brunel, Isambard Kingdom 43
Bryson, Bill 75
Burgess, Anthony: *A Clockwork Orange* 91
Burrows, Abe 112
Burton, Richard 100
Bush, George W. 63
'Bushes and Briars' 117
Byrd, William 18, 64, 123
Byron, George Gordon, Lord 4

C
Cage, John: *4'33"* 98
'Camptown Races' 57
Capercaillie (band) 124
Cherubini, Luigi 35
Chopin, Frédéric 22, 114
Cimarosa, Domenico 63
Clarke, Jeremiah 50
Clash, The 110
Clementi, Muzio 35, 111
Coates, Eric: *Dam Busters March, The* 118
Cole, Natalie 20
Cole, Nat King 20

Collins, Phil 111
Collins, William 4
Confucius 3
Cooke, Deryck 93, 99
Copland, Aaron 99
   Quiet City 105
Coppola, Francis Ford: *Apocalypse Now* 91
Costello, Elvis 129
Coward, Noël 115
   Private Lives 117
Cranmer, Thomas 131
Crotch, William 91
Czerny, Carl 35

D
Darmstadt 106, 135
Darwin, Charles 5, 32
Darwin, Erasmus 5
Davies, Peter Maxwell 108, 124
Davis, Carl: *Pride and Prejudice* (TV music) 104
Davis, Miles 110
Day, John 125
Debussy, Claude 96, 129
   La fille aux cheveux de lin 97
Deicide (band): 'Fuck Your God' 63
Delius, Frederick 89
Desert Island Discs 50
Dickens, Charles 78
Dryden, John 3
Duncan, Ronald 116
Dunstaple, John 78
Dušek, František 34, 86
Dury, Ian 115
Dylan, Bob 34, 64
   'Mr Tambourine Man' 118

E
EastEnders (TV theme) 73
Eliot, T. S. 6
Elgar, Edward 32, 68, 83, 98, 104, 118

Elizabeth I, Queen 78
Ellington, Duke 103, 104

F
Feuilles mortes, Les (song) 113
Feuer, Cy 112
Finzi, Gerald 88
Flanders and Swann: 'The Slow
    Train' 129
Fletcher, Andrew, of Saltoun 66
'Fly Me to the Moon' 113
'For He's a Jolly Good Fellow' 62
Forster, E. M. 129
'Frère Jacques' 50
Fukuyama, Francis 98
Fux, Johann Joseph 78

G
Gaga, Lady: 'Poker Face' 113, 114
Gershwin, George 22, 80
    Rhapsody in Blue 87, 105, 110, 122
    'They Can't Take That Away
        From Me' 49
Gesualdo, Carlo 110
Gilbert, W. S. 124
Gladwell, Malcolm 35
Glass, Philip 127
Glock, William 106
'God Save the Queen' (national
    anthem) 49, 64
Goehr, Lydia 31
Goethe, Johann Wolfgang 83, 90
Goldoni, Carlo 85
Green Day 111
'Greensleeves' 18, 64
Greenwood, Jonny 122
'Groovy Kind of Love' 111

H
Hamilton, Emma 63
Hammerstein, Oscar II 124
Hamilton-Paterson, James 59

Handel, George Frederic 22, 40, 73,
    90, 107
    Messiah 74
Hartley, L. P. 73
Harvey, Jonathan 97
Haydn, Josef 86, 104, 118
    The Creation 72
    Oxford Symphony 13
    String Quartet in F, op. 77,
        no. 2 46
Haydn, Michael 86
Hendrix, Jimi 50
Hildegard of Bingen 72
Hobbes, Thomas 12, 78
Holst, Gustav 40: 'Jupiter' (from
    The Planets) 50
Howard, Trevor 50

I
Iamblichus 2
Ives, Charles 128

J
Jagger, Mick 73
Janáček, Leoš 55
Jeans, James 79
'Call Me Maybe' 71
Joel, Billy 115
    'Piano Man' 118
John, Elton: 'Yellow Brick Road'
    45, 113
Johnson, Celia 50
Johnson, Dr Samuel 11, 78
Jones, Aled 20
Joplin, Scott 117

K
Kaku, Michio 130, 131
Keats, John 23, 77
Kerman, Joseph 31
Kern, Jerome 117
'Killing Me Softly' 118

INDEX

King, Martin Luther 100
Kings Singers, The 111
Koresh, David 63
Korngold, Erich 40
Kuehl, Lt-Col Dan 62

L

language 25
Larkin, Philip 109
Le Corbusier 129
Led Zeppelin 41
Lean, David 50
Lennon, John 112
Levy, John 57
Ligeti, György 122, 124
'Lillibullero' 59
Lloyd, Marie 32
Lloyd Webber, Andrew 116
Locke, John 67
Loesser, Frank: *Guys and Dolls* 116
Loussier, Jacques 49
Lucas, George 40
Lucier, Alvin: *I am sitting in a room* 98
Ludford, Nicholas 72

M

MacMillan, James 97, 121, 124
Mahler, Alma (née Schindler) 36
Mahler, Gustav 36, 104
    Symphony no. 1 50
Manilow, Barry 63
Marais, Marin 72
'Marching through Georgia' 59
Martin, Ernest 112
Martin, George 81, 125
Mayerl, Billy 76
McCartney, Paul 69, 79, 112, 122
Mendelssohn, Felix 35, 107, 129
    Hebrides Overture 91
Messiaen, Olivier 65, 106, 107, 127

Milhaud, Darius 80: *La Création du Monde* 122
Miller, Mitch 63
Mitchell, Donald 47, 127
Monteverdi, Claudio 72, 106, 108, 110
Morgan, Annie 57
Morley, Thomas 59, 78
Mozart, Wolfgang Amadeus 5, 15, 17, 18, 30, 33, 34, 35, 37, 43, 45, 70, 73, 74, 76, 77, 78, 86, 106, 107, 108, 124, 124
    The Marriage of Figaro 40, 114, 115
    Piano Sonata no. 5 in G major 42

N

Napoleon 60, 62
Nelson, Horatio, Admiral Lord 63
New Seekers 5
Nielsen, Carl 106
Niles, John Jacob 57
Nono, Luigi 106, 125
notation 15, 25

O

'One-Note Samba' 114
Opie, Iona and Peter 67
Orff, Carl: *Carmina Burana* 72

P

Page, Jimmy 41
Palestrina, Giovanni Pierluigi da 33, 97, 105
Parker, Charlie 109
Parker, Matthew 90
Pärt, Arvo 127
Petrucci, Ottaviano 125
Piazzolla, Astor 39
Pink: 'The Truth About Love' 115
plainsong 25
Plant, Robert 41
Plato 2, 130

Porter, Cole 33
   'Every Time We Say Goodbye' 114
   'Night and Day' 114
prehistory 25
Presley, Elvis 34
Prince 76
Proust, Marcel 91
Puccini, Giacomo 107
   Turandot 31
Purcell, Henry 33, 35, 72, 90, 104, 106, 114
   Dido and Aeneas 41
Pythagoras 2, 5, 9, 78, 130

R

Rachmaninoff, Sergei 35
   Piano Concerto no. 2 50
Rautavaara, Einojuhani 89
recording 20
Rhodes, James 35
Rodgers, Richard 124
Rolling Stones, The: 'It's Only Rock 'n' Roll (But I Like It)' 81
Rosen, Charles 92, 109, 123
Ross, Alex 77
Rossini, Gioachino 84, 86, 124
Runyon, Damon 112

S

Saint-Saëns, Camille 91
Salieri, Antonio 40
Schiller, Friedrich 65
Schoenberg, Arnold 18, 31, 47, 78, 84, 106, 107, 108, 109, 110, 123
   A Survivor from Warsaw 65
Scholes, Percy 41, 49
Schubert, Franz 77
Schumann, Robert: 'Der Dichter spricht' 97
Scott, Walter 5
Scriabin, Alexander 11

Sex Pistols, The: 'God Save The Queen' 64
Shaffer, Peter 40
Shakespeare, William: *Julius Caesar* 1
   The Merchant of Venice 1
Sharp, Cecil 57, 71
Shostakovich, Dmitri: *Symphony no. 5* 64
Sibelius, Jean 35
Sinatra, Nancy 63
Sousa, John Philip 117
Spector, Phil 125
Spring-Rice, Cecil 50
Stafford Smith, Clive 63
Stanford, Charles Villiers 39
'Star-Spangled Banner' 50
Stockhausen, Karlheinz 106, 125, 130
Stornoway (band) 89, 124
Strauss, Johann II 117
   The Blue Danube 85
Strauss, Richard 84, 106
   Salome 31
   Till Eulenspiegels lustige Streiche 46
Stravinsky, Igor 37, 40, 73, 74, 81, 84
Sullivan, Arthur 117, 124

T

'Takeda Lullaby' 56
'Take Five' 113
Tallis, Thomas 45, 90
   'In ieiunio et fletu' 44
Taverner, John 121, 127
Tchaikovsky, Pyotr Ilyich: Symphony no. 6 *(Pathétique)* 81
Telemann, Georg Philipp 59
Terfel, Bryn 87
Thackray, Jake 115
Thatcher, Margaret 35
'There Must Be An Angel' 114
Tippett, Michael 5, 105, 112
Titanic (film score) 85

INDEX

Turnage, Mark-Anthony: *Greek* 122
Turner, J. M. W. 91

U
U2 (band) 127

V
Varèse, Edgard 129
Vaughan Williams, Ralph 12, 39, 55, 83, 123, 124
Verdi, Giuseppe 89, 107
Vivaldi, Antonio 89

W
Wagner, Richard 84, 87, 91, 106, 115, 125
Walton, William: *Henry V* (film music) 85

Warner, Marina 67
Waters, Roger 122
Wesley, Charles 91
Whitacre, Eric 126
Whiteman, Paul 110
Williams, John 40
Williams, Robbie 32
Woan, Ronald 69
Wodehouse, P. G. 117
Wood, Henry 111
'World in Union' 50
Wren, Christopher 78

X
Xenakis, Iannis 130

Y
'Ye Banks and Braes' 56

IDEAS IN PROFILE
SMALL INTRODUCTIONS TO BIG TOPICS

Ideas in Profile is a landmark series that offers concise and entertaining
introductions to topics that matter.

ALREADY PUBLISHED

The Ancient World Jerry Toner
Art in History Martin Kemp
Criticism Catherine Belsey
Geography Carl Lee and Danny Dorling
Politics David Runciman
Shakespeare Paul Edmondson
Social Theory William Outhwaite
Theories of Everything Frank Close
Truth Simon Blackburn

FORTHCOMING

Conservatism Roger Scruton
Feminism Deborah Cameron
Language Alexandra Aikhenvald
Socialism Mark Stears